EXECUTIVE EDITORS
Sarah Galbraith, Alan Doan,
Jenny Doan, David Mifsud

MANAGING EDITOR
Natalie Earnheart

CREATIVE DIRECTOR
Christine Ricks

PHOTOGRAPHER
BPD Studios

CONTRIBUTING PHOTOGRAPHERS
Mike Brunner, Lauren Dorton

VIDEOGRAPHER
Jake Doan

TECHNICAL WRITER
Edie McGinnis

TECHNICAL EDITOR
Denise Lane

PATTERN LAYOUT DESIGN
Ally Simmons

PROJECT DESIGN TEAM
Natalie Earnheart, Jenny Doan,
Sarah Galbraith

AUTHOR OF THE FAIR THIEF
Steve Westover

CONTRIBUTING COPYWRITERS
Jenny Doan, Natalie Earnheart, Christine Ricks,
Katie Mifsud, Camille Maddox, Nichole Spravzoff,
Edie McGinnis

COPY EDITOR
Nichole Spravzoff

CONTRIBUTING PIECERS
Jenny Doan, Natalie Earnheart, Carol Henderson,
Cindy Morris, Denise Lane, Janice Richardson

CONTRIBUTING QUILTERS
Jamey Stone-Manager, Sarah Richardson-Lead,
Angela Wilson, Linda Frump, Debbie Elder, Betty
Bates, Rachel Hale, Karla Zinkand, Jan Meek,
Chelsea White, Debbie Allen, Charlene Ensz, Jamee
Gilgour, Stephanie Weaver, Jennifer Dowling,
Christine Atteberry-Pulley, Kara Snow-Night Assist
Manager, Devin Ragle, Nikki LaPiana, Rachael
Joyce, Bruce Van Iperen, Michaela Butterfield,
Francesca Flemming, Aaron Crawford, Ethan Lucas,
Lyndia Lovell, Cyera Cottrill, Natasha Green-Mahler

BINDING SPECIALISTS
Deloris Burnett
Bernice Kelly

PRINTING COORDINATOR
Rob Stoebener

PRINTING SERVICES
Walsworth Print Group
803 South Missouri
Marceline, MO 64658

CONTACT US
Missouri Star Quilt Company
114 N Davis
Hamilton, Mo. 64644
888-571-1122
info@missouriquiltco.com

W9-AAZ-020

content

*Oops! Sometimes we make mistakes.
To find corrections to every issue of Block
go to:* **www.msqc.co/corrections**

hello
from MSQC

Winter is heading our way soon and this time of the year just calls for a change of pace. I love settling in and making the whole house feel cozier. Stoking the fire, sipping some cocoa, and watching the snow fall feels so magical. Heading toward the end of the year can also be pretty hectic with all the festivities, so it's easy to get burned out if we're not careful to pace ourselves. The other day my daughter, Sarah, said to me, "I need to go to the spaspital." Spaspital? I wondered. "Yeah, it's like a hospital, but for people who just need a trip to the spa to recover. It could be a place where you can check in and just get taken care of. You get a massage, a delicious meal, and you never have to do the dishes!" Wow, doesn't that sound amazing? I pictured all my worries floating away as I got a pedicure, wrapped in a white fluffy robe. And you know, that dream isn't too far-fetched. We all need to take a moment every now and then to slow down and enjoy life.

One of my biggest challenges is learning how to take better care of myself. I can find time for everyone and everything else, but there's rarely enough time left over for me. And I'm not the only one. I see this a lot, especially with quilters. So much of what we do is for others. By nature, quilters tend to be generous, thoughtful people, but If there is one thing I know, it's that we can't keep giving when there's nothing left to give. We all need to find something that replenishes our energy and take the time to do it—both for the sake of the people who need us and for ourselves! So let's begin right now to take better care of ourselves and watch out for those around us who could use a reprieve as well. If you're wondering where to start, why not wrap up in a warm, cozy quilt and treat yourself to this issue of Block and maybe a cookie or two.

JENNY DOAN
MISSOURI STAR QUILT CO

winter **blues**

I can hardly wait for the holidays to come. After Halloween I'm usually hard-pressed to jump right past Thanksgiving and into Christmas. But after the festivities are over and the decorations are all put away it's hard not to get a little blue. Winter sets in and all my body wants to do is climb into bed and sleep until spring.

To combat this urge to hibernate, I've adopted a couple of ways to enjoy this chilly season more fully. I love being outdoors, so I've taken up snowshoeing. The peace of hiking along a trail and the sound of my feet crunching on top of the snow is a truly rejuvenating experience.

Long winter nights also provide ample time to begin new projects. I take advantage of this time and begin a new quilt or work on a new skill. It definitely helps boost my mood and leaves me feeling satisfied and happy.

Whatever your experience is with the winter blues, try picking up a new hobby to lift your spirits and get you through the long winter. My guess is you'll be glad you did!

CHRISTINE RICKS
MSQC Creative Director, BLOCK MAGAZINE

PRINTS

FBY47645 Vintage Daydream - Vintage Words Pink by Design by Dani for Riley Blake
SKU: C5562-PINK

FBY35287 Whisper - Puffs Soft Blue by Victoria Johnson for Windham Fabrics
SKU: 41361-3

FBY41930 Dapper Wovens - Check is in the Mail Wine Stain by Luke for Moda Fabrics
SKU: 12250 13

FBY45152 Feedsack - Outline Floral Yellow by Whistler Studios for Windham Fabrics
SKU: 41870-3

FBY35432 Garden Days - Garden Tile Dark Green by Cheryl Haynes for Benartex
SKU: 1007644B

FBY28825 Acorn Forest - Sorbet Trees Yardage by Wendy Kendall for Robert Kaufman
SKU: AWY-15626-239

SOLIDS

FBY1679 Bella Solids - Pale Pink from Moda Fabrics
SKU: 9900 26

FBY12175 Bella Solids - Steel by Moda Fabrics
SKU: 9900 184

FBY12182 Bella Solids - Eggplant by Moda Fabrics
SKU: 9900 205

FBY12208 Bella Solids - Saffron by Moda Fabrics
SKU: 9900 232

FBY12210 Bella Solids - Evergreen by Moda Fabrics
SKU: 9900 234

FBY1126 Bella Solids - Navy by Moda Fabrics
SKU: 9900 20

baby
kisses

When people find out you're a quilter, they expect certain things of you. Oh, you'd like a quilt? Handsewn? King size? And you need it by tomorrow? Some expectations are easier to meet than others, like baby quilts. With just a couple of charm packs, I can put together a baby quilt in no time! Everybody hopes that the quilter they know will make them a baby quilt, and that's one thing I love to do for new babies in the family. We've got twenty one grandchildren to date, and I traditionally make each one a baby quilt at first and then a larger one when they move to a big bed.

Baby quilts are fun, easy projects to take on. Almost any quilt pattern can work for a baby. Just take your favorite block and add borders until it's the right size for wrapping up a little one, and voila, you've got a baby quilt! For this Baby Kisses quilt, we put together four blocks and it turned out be the perfect size.

I also love creating a quilt with the recipient in mind, and that's especially fun when you're making it for a cute baby. And boy,

For the tutorial and everything need you to make this quilt visit:
www.msqc.co/blockearlywinter16

my grandkids were all cute babies! I guess I might be a little biased, but to me they are absolutely adorable!

Now, cute babies are fun to quilt for, but between you and me, I enjoy them even more when they're a bit bigger. Send 'em to me when they're two and sassy! I just love the things they say. The other day my grandson, Gid, asked me if I was going to get security cameras for my house. Stunned, I asked him why I would need security cameras.

"What if someone breaks into your house?" he asked me.

"Why would someone want to break into my house?" I asked.

Gid looked around and said, "Well maybe someone else out there likes old stuff."

My face must have registered the surprise I felt, because his sister, Ashelyn, trying to come to my rescue said, "Or chickens, Grandma, they could like chickens." I guess I like chickens and old stuff! Kids sure say the darndest things.

materials

makes a 51" X 51" quilt

QUILT TOP
- 2 packages 5" squares
- 1¾ yards background fabric - includes inner border

OUTER BORDER
- ¾ yard

BINDING
- ½ yard

BACKING
- 3¼ yards - vertical seam(s)

SAMPLE QUILT
- **Garden Girl** by Zoe Pearn for Riley Blake Designs

1 cut

From the background fabric, cut:

- (16) 2½" strips across the width of the fabric. Subcut 9 strips into 2½" squares for a **total of 144.** Set the remaining strips aside for sashing and borders.

2 mark

On the reverse side of the 2½" background squares, draw a line or press a crease from corner to corner once on the diagonal. This marks your sewing line. **2A**

2A

3A

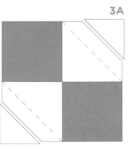

3 snowball corners

3B

Select (64) 5" squares and place a 2½" background square on 2 opposite corners of the square with right sides facing. Sew on the marked sewing line. Trim the excess fabric away ¼" from the sewn seam and press. 3A

Select 16 of the squares you've snowballed. Place another 2½" marked background square on 1 of the remaining corners and sew on the marked line. Trim the excess fabric away ¼" from the sewn seam and press. Set these "center units" aside to use in the middle of each block. 3B

4 block construction

4A

Each block is made up of **4 rows** of **4 units.**

Make rows 1 and 4 by sewing 4 units together as shown. 4A

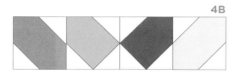

4B

Make rows 2 and 3 by sewing 4 units together as shown. Notice that the units used in the middle of each row are the center units that each have 3 snowballed corners. 4B

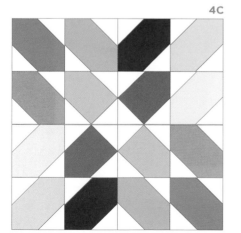

4C

Sew the 4 rows together to complete the block. **Make 4 blocks.** 4C

Block Size: 18" finished

5 layout and sew

Cut (1) 2½" square and (4) 18½" increments from (2) 2½" background strips you have set aside. We are using the 18½" strips for our sashing rectangles.

Sew a block to either side of 1 sashing rectangle to make the top row. Repeat for the bottom row. 5A

To make the center sashing row, sew a sashing rectangle to either side of the background 2½" square. 5B

Sew a row of sashed blocks to either side of the center sashing strip to complete the center of the quilt. 5C

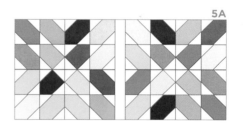

5A

5B

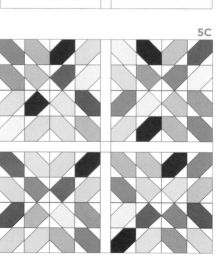

5C

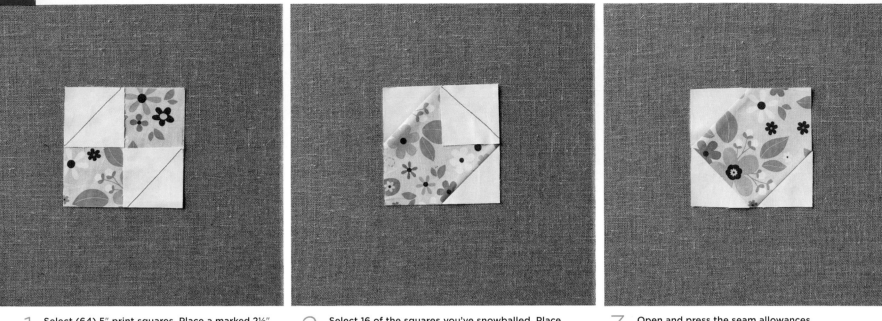

1 Select (64) 5″ print squares. Place a marked 2½″ background square on two opposing corners with right sides facing. Sew on the marked line. Trim the excess fabric ¼″ away from the sewn seam and press.

2 Select 16 of the squares you've snowballed. Place another 2½″ marked background square on 1 of the remaining corners and sew on the marked line. Trim the excess fabric ¼″ away from the sewn seam.

3 Open and press the seam allowances toward the print fabric.

4 Arrange the snowballed units into rows. You'll need two rows made as shown in the top row and two rows made as shown in the bottom row. Sew all four rows together to make one block. You'll need 4 blocks for your quilt.

6 inner border

Sew the remaining (5) 2½"
background strips together end-to-
end to make one long strip. Trim the
borders from this strip.

Refer to Borders (pg. 100) in the
Construction Basics to measure and
cut the inner borders. The strips are
approximately 38½" for the sides and
approximately 42½" for the top and
bottom.

7 outer border

Cut (5) 5" strips across the width of
the fabric. Sew the strips together end-
to-end to make one long strip. Trim the
borders from this strip.

Refer to Borders (pg. 100) in the
Construction Basics to measure and
cut the outer borders. The strips are
approximately 42½" for the sides and
approximately 51½" for the top and
bottom.

8 quilt and bind

Layer the quilt with batting and
backing and quilt. After the quilting is
complete, square up the quilt and trim
away all excess batting and backing.
Add binding to complete the quilt.
See Construction Basics (pg. 101) for
binding instructions.

For the tutorial and everything you need to make this quilt visit: www.msqc.co/blockearlywinter16

butterfly
blossoms

Blossoming into who we are meant to be is a lifelong process and we can't do it alone. As we look to special people in our lives for help and encouragement, their examples can teach us how to challenge ourselves and improve. Throughout my life I've been privileged to learn from some wonderful men and women, and as I've tried to pattern my life after them, I've become a better version of myself.

Beth, a sweet lady in my church congregation, was the first of many such mentors. As a kid, I loved to be the center of attention and was always ready with a clever comment or funny joke, but I did have the tendency to get a tad off-color now and then. The older I got, however, the more I worried about being inappropriate. That's when I started looking to Beth for help. She was so lovely and full of class; her words and actions always seemed above reproach. I decided to use Beth as a barometer for my big, hard-to-tame personality. Before I said anything, I would pause and ask myself, "Would Beth think this is funny?" Believe it or not, it really helped! Beth wasn't a perfect person, but she taught me to think before I speak and I'll always be grateful to her.

Then, when I was in my early thirties, I met another wonderful mentor, Bruce, who was the leader of our church congregation. Bruce was one of the most loving, talented people I have ever known, and not only did he teach me how to love more selflessly, he taught me to be bold and share my talents. I remember sitting in church one Christmas. It was time for the closing song and the organist began to play "Joy to the World." Suddenly, without invitation, Bruce walked up to the front of the chapel, opened the lid of the piano, and began to play along with the organ. It was a dazzlingly beautiful duet. We knew it was his gift to us, and when the congregation joined in, we sang with the feeling of a hundred heavenly choirs. How thankful we were that Bruce was willing to create such a magical moment for us! I think back on that experience whenever I need a little nudge to let my own light shine.

Later in life, I met another mentor named Audrey. I had the opportunity to care for Audrey in her old age. She was very ill and required quite a lot of assistance. It was hard work and took some sacrifice on my part, but it was a joy to spend time with her and she became a close friend. When she finally lost her battle with cancer, I was heartbroken, but I came to better understand how much love we can develop for those we help. Because of that experience, I've been more willing to reach out to others, even when it seems inconvenient or difficult.

In our lives, dear friends come and go. If we're lucky, they leave behind a bit of themselves that will stay with us forever. No matter where we begin, we all have the potential to learn and grow if we are willing. Keep blossoming my friends!

materials
makes a 56" X 66" quilt

QUILT TOP
- 2 packages 5" print squares
- 2 packages 5" background squares
- ¾ yard background – includes sashing strips and inner border.

OUTER BORDER
- 1½ yards

BINDING
- ¾ yard

BACKING
- 3¾ yards - horizontal seam(s)

OTHER SUPPLIES
- MSQC Periwinkle Template

OPTIONAL
- Glue Stick

SAMPLE QUILT
- **Daisy Blue** by Flaurie & Finch for RJR Fabrics

1 cut

Choose 80 of the 5" print squares. From each, cut 1 periwinkle shape using the MSQC Periwinkle Template.

From the remaining print squares, cut (12) 1½" squares. Set the squares aside to use as cornerstones in the sashing.

From the background fabric, cut:

- (8) 1½" strips across the width of the fabric. Subcut the strips into (31) 1½" X 9½" rectangles. Set the rectangles aside to use for sashing. Use the remaining fabric for the inner borders.

2 prepare the pieces

Turn and press a ¼" seam allowance under on the 2 longer edges of the periwinkle pieces. If necessary, use a little glue to hold the seam allowances down. The glue is especially handy on the corners of the pieces. **2A**

2A

3A

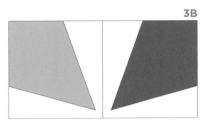

3B

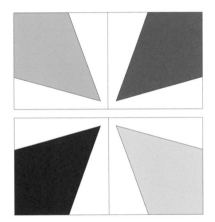

3 sew

Align the corner portion of the periwinkle shape with the corner of the 5" background square. Either pin the periwinkle shape to the background or use a few dabs of glue to hold it in place.

Appliqué the piece to the 5" background square using a blind hemstitch, small zigzag, or blanket stitch. You only need to appliqué the portion that stretches into the 5" square. The remaining two short edges will catch in the seam allowances. **Make 4.** 3A

Sew the 4 pieces together in a 4-patch formation. Sew 2 pieces together as shown to make one half of the block, **make 2.** Sew the 2 halves together to complete the block. **Make 20 blocks.** 3B **Block Size:** 9" Finished

4 lay out the blocks

Lay out the blocks in rows. Each row has **4 blocks** across and there are **5 rows.** When you are happy with the arrangement, begin sewing the row together. Add a sashing rectangle between each block. 4A

Before you sew the rows together, make 4 sashing strips to go between each row. Sew a cornerstone to a sashing rectangle. Add another sashing rectangle. Continue on in this manner until you have sewn 4 rectangles and 3 cornerstones together. **Make 4.** 4B

Sew the rows and the sashing strips together to complete the center of the quilt.

5 inner border

Cut (5) 1½" strips across the width of the fabric. Sew the strips together end-to-end to make one long strip. Trim the borders from this strip.

Refer to Borders (pg. 100) in the Construction Basics to measure and cut the inner borders. The strips are approximately 49½" for the sides and approximately 41½" for the top and bottom.

6 outer border

Cut (6) 8" strips across the width of the fabric. Sew the strips together end-to-end to make one long strip. Trim the borders from this strip.

4A

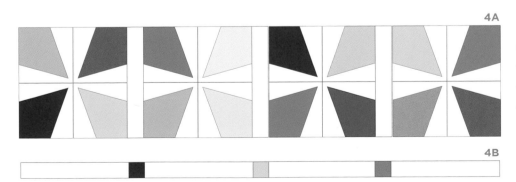

4B

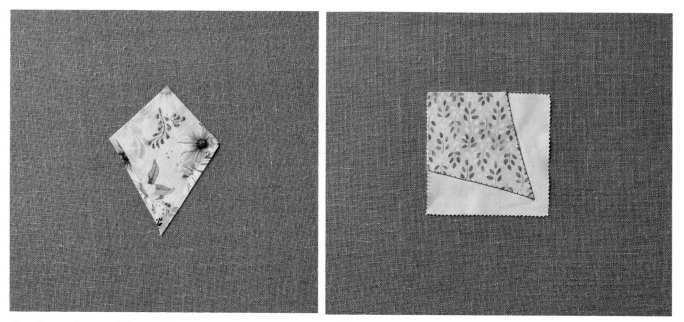

1 Turn and press a ¼″ seam allowance under on the two longest edges of the periwinkle pieces.

2 Appliqué a prepared periwinkle shape to a 5″ background square using a blind hemstitch, zigzag, or blanket stitch. Make four per block.

3 Sew 2 pieces together as shown to make one half of the block. Make 2.

4 Sew the two halves together to complete the block. Make 20 blocks.

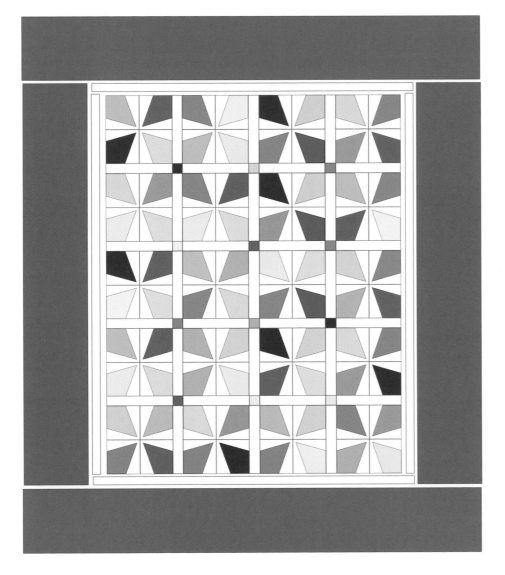

Refer to Borders (pg. 100) in the Construction Basics to measure and cut the outer borders. The strips are approximately 51½" for the sides and approximately 56½" for the top and bottom.

7 quilt and bind

Layer the quilt with batting and backing and quilt. After the quilting is complete, square up the quilt and trim away all excess batting and backing. Add binding to complete the quilt. See Construction Basics (pg. 101) for binding instructions.

desert
sunset

Great things can happen over the phone. News of a new baby, a long chat with a dear friend, meandering conversations between loved ones that make it hard to hang up. I know a sweet older couple that have a tradition of calling each of their kids and grandkids on their birthday and singing "Happy Birthday" over the phone in two-part harmony! Remember when calling friends and family around the country was so expensive because of those pesky long-distance charges? Now calling all over the U.S. and beyond is as easy as calling down the street.

I've had a lot of great phone calls in my life, but I'm going to tell you about one I'll never forget. One day I got a call from these three nice guys in Arizona. They have a shop called 3 Dudes Quilting and they said, "We love what you did with half-square triangles. Guess what we did …" I was rapt as I listened to their explanation of a new quilt pattern that was absolutely genius.

For the tutorial and everything
you need to make this quilt visit:
www.msqc.co/blockearlywinter16

It all began with a couple rolls of 2½″ strips. They had sewn strips together into sets of four and cut them into squares. Then they took two squares of strips and placed them one on top of the other, one vertically and one horizontally, with right sides together. The magic happened after the outside edge was sewn, just like we do with half-square triangles. Then the squares were cut diagonally, from corner to corner. When you opened up the four new blocks, the result was fantastic!

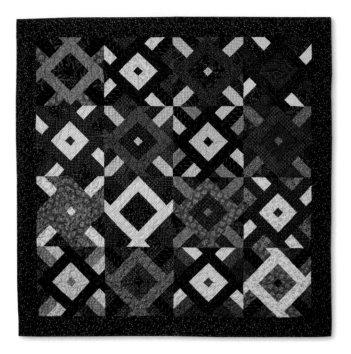

Well, I was stunned. What an amazing idea! Then my brain went wild. I started thinking about all the possibilities: you could change the number of strips, change the color placement, change the sizes of the stripes, rotate the blocks in different directions, and much more! There are so many things you can do with this pattern. I love it when someone shares an idea and magic happens. I will forever be grateful for these three dudes who picked up the phone and opened my mind up to new possibilities!

materials

makes a 59" X 59" quilt

QUILT TOP
- 1 roll of 2½" x 42" strips

OUTER BORDER
- ¾ yard

BINDING
- ¾ yard

BACKING
- 3¾ yards - vertical seam(s)

SAMPLE QUILT
- **Katie's Cupboard** by Kim Diehl for Henry Glass Fabrics

1 make strip sets

Sew 5 assorted strips together to make 1 strip set. **Make 8.** Cut each strip set into (4) 10½" squares. Stack the matching squares together. **1A**

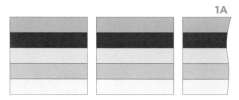

2 sew

Layer 2 matching squares together with right sides facing. The strips on one of the squares need to be vertical while the strips on the other square need to run horizontally. **2A**

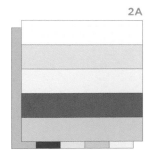

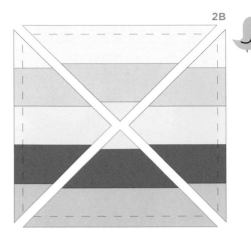

2B

Note: *Make sure your squares are always oriented in the same direction, otherwise your blocks may not match.*

Sew all the way around the perimeter of the squares using a ¼" seam allowance. Cut each square from corner to corner twice on the diagonal. Open to reveal 2 sets of 2 matching block units. Repeat for a total of **2 sets** of **4 matching block units**. 2B

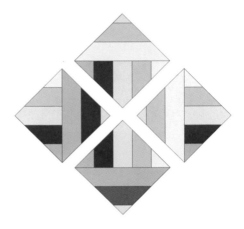

2C

Lay out 4 matching block units and stitch them together to complete 1 block. **Make 16 blocks.** 2C

Block Size: 13" Finished

3 lay out blocks

Lay out the blocks in **4 rows** with each row having **4 blocks.** Sew each row together and press the seam allowances in the odd numbered rows toward the right and the even numbered rows toward the left. This will make the seam allowances nest and will make the corners easier to match up.

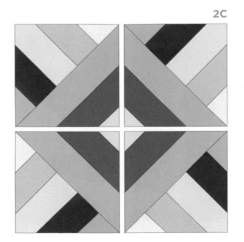

4 border

Cut (6) 4" strips across the width of the fabric. Sew the strips together end-to-end to make one long strip. Trim the borders from this strip.

Refer to Borders (pg. 100) in the Construction Basics to measure and cut the outer borders. The strips are approximately 52½" for the sides and approximately 59½" for the top and bottom.

5 quilt and bind

Layer the quilt with batting and backing and quilt. After the quilting is complete, square up the quilt and trim away all excess batting and backing. Add binding to complete the quilt. See Construction Basics (pg. 101) for binding instructions.

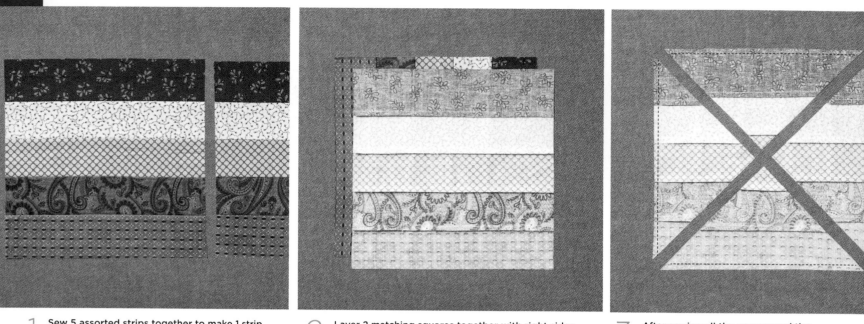

1 Sew 5 assorted strips together to make 1 strip set. Cut each strip set into (4) 10½″ squares. Stack the matching squares together.

2 Layer 2 matching squares together with right sides facing. The strips of one of the squares needs run vertically and the other, horizontally.

3 After sewing all the way around the perimeter of the squares using a ¼″ seam allowance, cut the sewn squares twice on the diagonal. Open to reveal 2 sets of 2 matching block units.

4 Lay out 4 matching block units and stitch them together to complete 1 block.

5 Lay out the blocks in rows of 4. When you are happy with the appearance, sew the rows together.

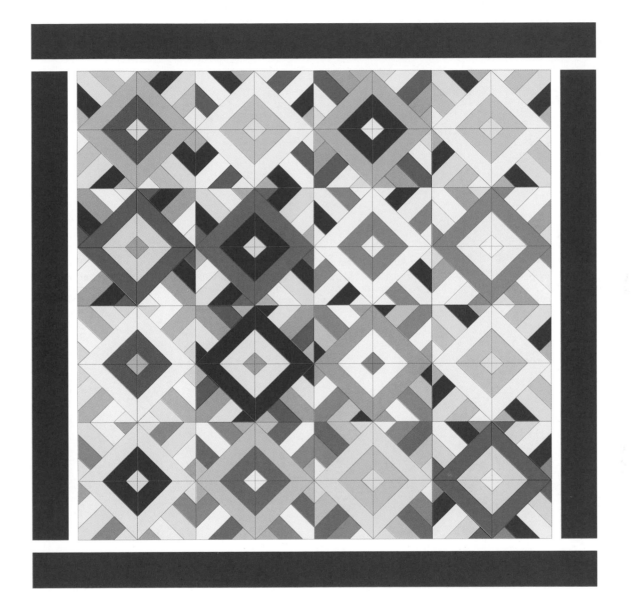

For the tutorial and everything you need to make this quilt visit: www.msqc.co/blockearlywinter16

diamond
dash

How much would you pay for an eight-carat diamond? If you said $8, you're in luck—as long as you have a sharp eye and an enormous amount of patience and good fortune. At Crater of Diamonds State Park in Murfreesboro, Arkansas, you can pay a small fee to search the grounds for diamonds. If you're lucky enough to find one, it's yours to keep!

Millions of years ago, a volcanic eruption scattered gems throughout the area. Today, visitors to the park spend hours upon hours carefully sifting through rocks and dirt, hoping to spot just a speck of sparkle. Success is rare, but just last year someone unearthed an 8.52 carat stone! Since 1906, a total of 75,000 diamonds have been discovered, some as

large as 40 carats. I've never had the pleasure of hunting for diamonds, but I have done my fair share of digging for gold. I did grow up in gold rush territory, after all.

When I was a young girl, there was a great birthday party venue in my hometown, Salinas, California. It was called Happy Valley Birthday Park, and it was the coolest place to go! Although it was relatively small, the layout was fantastic. There were plenty of swings, slides, and other playground equipment, and they even had bikes that could be ridden around the park. But my favorite feature of all was the gold mine.

The mine was situated right in the center of the park, and kids could actually go inside to pan for gold. A guide took us hiking into what seemed like a very deep, very dark mine, and then we were allowed to dig for "real" golden nuggets! I'm sure it wasn't quite as dramatic as I remember, but for my seven-year-old self, it was a grand adventure.

I've always had a great imagination and while panning for gold in that deep, dark mine, I became a pirate, searching for gold doubloons that had been hidden long ago and marked with an X on a ragged treasure map. I never did find anything, but the search was the fun part anyway. In life I like to enjoy the whole journey, not just the destination, that way I'm rarely disappointed! Whether it's a genuine diamond or a handful of fool's gold, there's just nothing as exhilarating as searching for treasure.

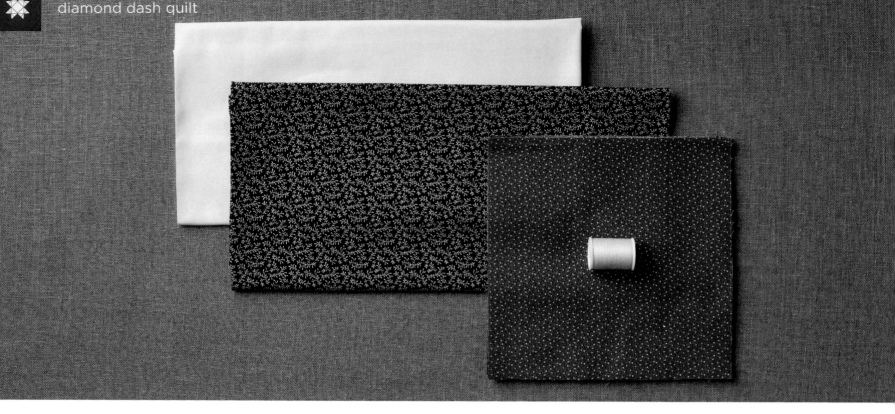

materials

makes a 77" x 81" quilt

QUILT TOP
- 1 package (42 ct.) 10" squares

SNOWBALLED CORNERS, SASHING STRIPS, & INNER BORDER
- 1¾ yards solid fabric

OUTER BORDER
- 1½ yards

BINDING
- ¾ yard

BACKING
- 5 yards - vertical seam(s) (42" wide)

SAMPLE QUILT
- **Vine** for Windham Fabrics by The Henry Ford Collection

1 cut

Cut each 10" square in half for a total of (84) 5" x 10" rectangles.

From the solid fabric, cut:

- (6) 2½" strips across the width of the fabric.

Subcut the strips into:

- (84) 2½" squares.

2 sew

Fold each square in half once on the diagonal and press along the crease.

Sew a 2½" square to one corner of a rectangle, using the pressed crease as your sewing line. Trim the excess fabric ¼" away from the sewn seam.

2A

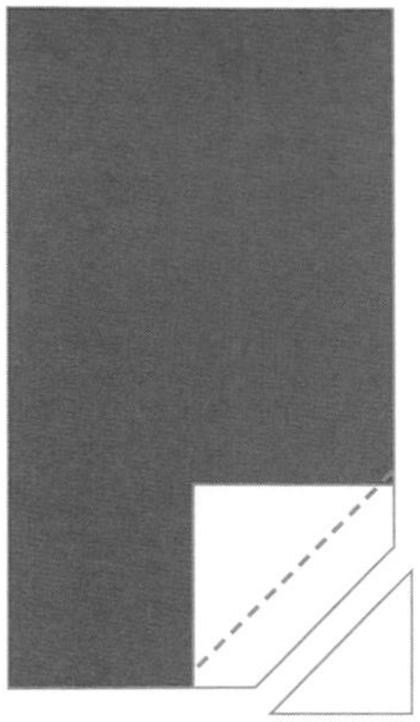

2B

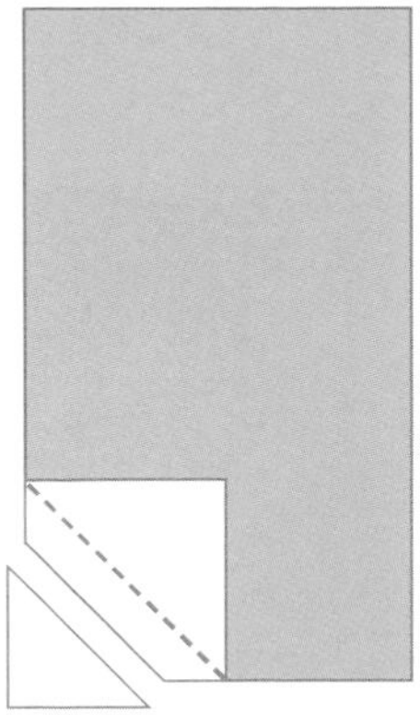

3A

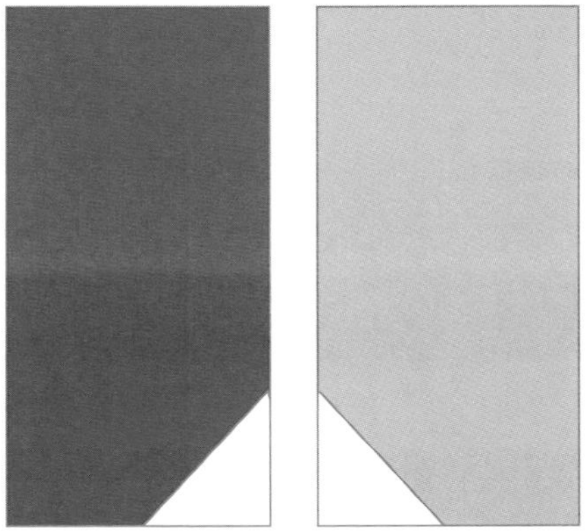

4A

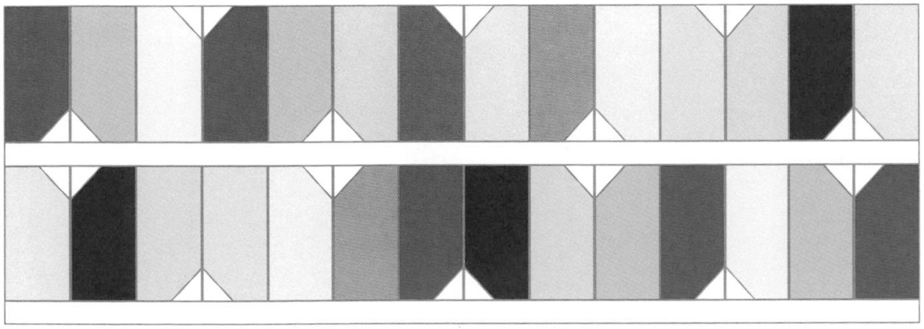

NOTE: *Half of the squares need to be sewn to the right side of a rectangle, the others to the left.* 2A 2B

3 make a block

Sew two rectangles together so the snowballed corners meet. **Make 42.** 3A

Block Size: 9" x 9½" Finished

4 arrange and sew

Sew the blocks together into rows containing 7 blocks. Notice that every other block is flipped 180 degrees. **Make 6 rows.**

Measure the length of the rows. Cut (8) 2½" strips across the width of the solid fabric. Sew the strips end-to-end, then cut (5) 2½" by your measurement of the row for sashing strips (approximately 63½"). Sew one to the bottom of each of the first 5 rows. Sew the rows together. 4A

5 inner borders

From the solid fabric, cut (7) 2½" x WOF strips. Sew the strips together end-to-end to make one long strip. Refer to Borders (pg. 100) in the Construction Basics to measure and cut the inner borders. The strips are approximately 67½" for the side borders and 67½" for the top and bottom.

6 outer borders

From the outer border fabric, cut (8) 5½" x WOF strips. Join the strips end-to-end to make one long strip.

Refer to Borders (pg. 100) in Construction Basics to measure and cut the outer borders. The strips are approximately 71½" for the sides and 77½" for the top and bottom.

1 Sew a 2½″ background square to a print 5″ x 10″ rectangle. *Note:* half of the background squares need to be sewn to the right side of a rectangle, the others to the left. Trim the excess fabric ¼″ away from the sewn seam.

2 Open and press the seam allowances toward the darker fabric.

3 Sew 2 rectangles together so the snowballed corners meet to complete 1 block.

4 Sew the blocks into rows, flipping every other block 180 degrees. Add sashing strips between each row.

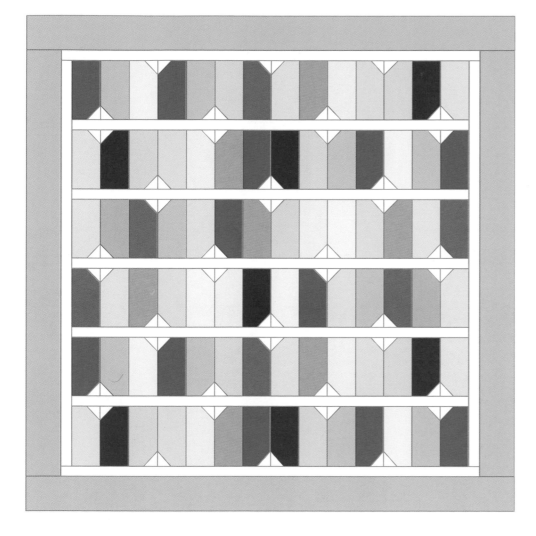

7 quilt and bind

Layer the quilt with backing and batting and quilt. After the quilting is complete, square up the quilt and trim away all excess batting and backing. Add binding to complete the quilt. See Construction Basics (pg. 101) for binding instructions.

flirty
table runner

I began collecting blue and white china as a young mother. I didn't care if the pieces were antique or valuable. If I found a pretty blue and white plate that wasn't too expensive, it was coming home with me! When my mother saw how much I was enjoying my collection, she gave me a beautiful blue and white plate to add to it, and she kept another exactly like it for herself.

I asked my husband to build a display shelf for my dishes, and every time I walked into the room, I looked up at my collection and smiled. One day, however, I came home and found that the shelf had crashed to the floor. My precious plate—the one my mother had given to me—was broken on the floor. Thankfully, I was able to glue it back together. It wasn't perfect, but it was still pretty.

A few years later, Mom gave me a tea set. She told me that my great-grandmother had carried it on her lap when she came on the boat from Sweden. For years that tea set was safely tucked away in my china cabinet. And then the unthinkable happened.

For the tutorial and everything
you need to make this quilt visit:
www.msqc.co/blockearlywinter16

Ron and I had gone out for a date and left the kids with a babysitter. For unknown reasons, that little gal let the kids ride their bikes inside the house, and then one of them had crashed into the china cabinet. The whole thing came crashing down and its contents were destroyed. Worst of all, my great-grandmother's tea set had shattered into a million tiny pieces. I tried to glue what I could, but it wasn't much. I swept up the remaining shards and put them in a sack that I shoved under the bed. I just couldn't bear to throw them away.

Years later, we were getting ready to move to a new home. The truck was almost loaded up and as they

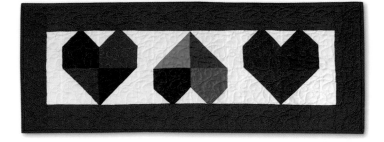

pulled out our bed, there in a bag were all the pieces of my beloved dishes. I'd practically forgotten about them. Later that night, after the kids were all settled down in their sleeping bags, I began to feel a bit nostalgic, so I pulled out my bag of broken dishes. There were so many pieces, but I was still hoping I could save something. After trying fruitlessly for about an hour, I wasn't able to put the puzzle back together. About that time one of my girls woke up and asked what I was doing. I looked at her with tears in my eyes and replied, "Gluing dishes."

Gluing dishes. Over the years that's become an oft-repeated phrase with so much meaning. When it feels like everything's falling apart and I'm just doing my best to hold it all together, that's when I say, "Don't mind me. I'm just over here gluing dishes."

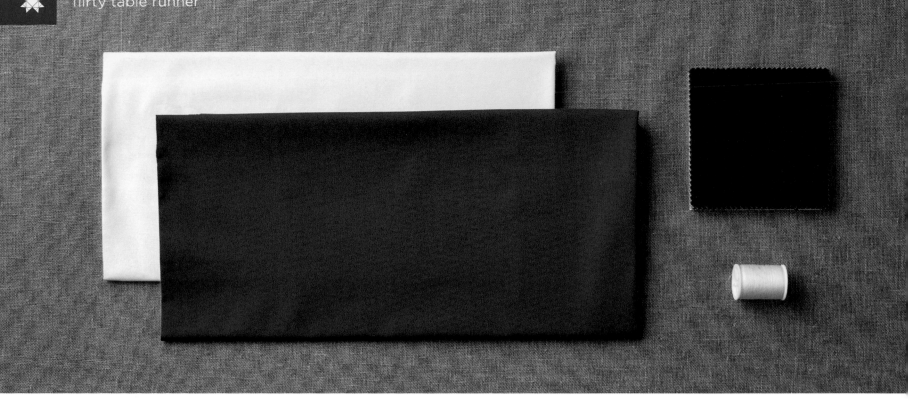

materials

makes a 42" X 16" table runner

TABLE RUNNER
- (12) 5" squares
- ½ yard background

BORDER AND BINDING
- ¾ yard

BACKING
- ¾ yards

SAMPLE QUILT
- **Paintbox Solids** by Elizabeth Hartman for Robert Kaufman

1 cut

From the background fabric, cut:

- (1) 5" x width of fabric strip – subcut the strip into (6) 5" squares.

- (1) 2½" x width of fabric strip – subcut the strip into (4) 2½" x 9½" rectangles.

- (1) 2¼" x width of fabric strip – subcut the strip into (12) 2¼" squares.

2 sew

Fold each of the 5" background squares once on the diagonal and press the

2A

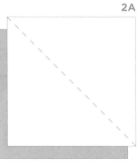

2B

crease in place to mark a sewing line. Place a creased background square atop a print 5″ square with right sides facing. Stitch on the sewing line then trim the excess fabric away ¼″ from the sewn seam. Repeat for the remaining squares. Open and press. Make a **total of 6** and set aside for the moment. We'll use these units for the bottom of the block. 2A

Fold each of the 2¼″ background squares once on the diagonal and press the crease in place to mark a sewing line. Place a creased 2¼″ background square on one corner of a 5″ print square with right sides facing. Stitch on the sewing line, then trim the excess fabric ¼″ away from the sewn seam. Repeat for the adjacent side of the square. **Make 6** and set aside for

the moment. These units will be used later on to make the top of the block. 2B

Lay out 2 bottom units and 2 top units. Sew the two top units together into a row and the two bottom units together into a row. Sew the rows together to complete the block. **Make 3.** 2C

Block Size: 9″ Finished

3 arrange and sew

Lay out the blocks. Add a 2½″ x 9½″ background rectangle between each block and at each end as shown on page 47. Sew the blocks and rectangles together to complete the center of the table runner.

4 border

Cut (3) 4″ strips across the width of the fabric. Sew the strips together end-to-end to make one long strip. Trim the borders from this strip.

Refer to Borders (pg. 100) in the Construction Basics to measure and cut the borders. The strips are approximately 42½″ for the top and bottom and approximately 9½″ for the sides.

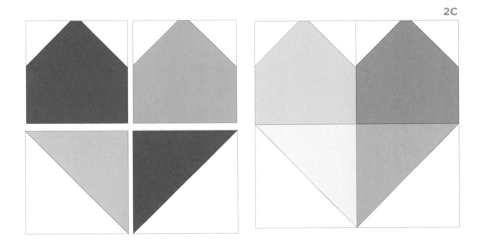

2C

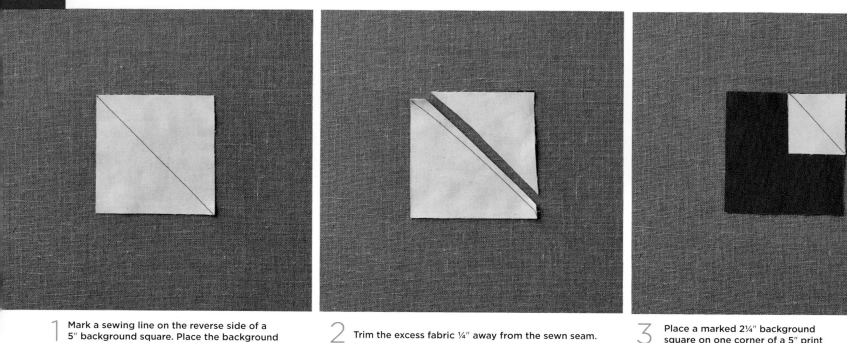

1 Mark a sewing line on the reverse side of a 5″ background square. Place the background square atop a print square with right sides facing. Sew on the marked line.

2 Trim the excess fabric ¼″ away from the sewn seam.

3 Place a marked 2¼″ background square on one corner of a 5″ print square with right sides facing. Sew on the drawn line.

4 Add another 2¼″ square to the adjacent corner of the 5″ print square and sew in place. Trim the excess fabric away ¼″ from the sewn seam.

5 Press the unit. Make 2 for each block.

6 Sew the 4 units together as shown to complete 1 block.

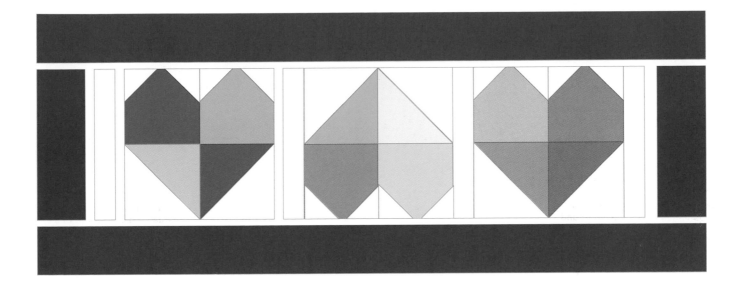

5 backing

Cut the backing fabric in half vertically. Sew the two pieces together along the short ends and trim to the desired size. Be sure your backing is at least 4" larger than the front on all 4 sides!

6 quilt and bind

Layer the quilt with batting and backing and quilt. After the quilting is complete, square up the quilt and trim away all excess batting and backing. Add binding to complete the quilt. See Construction Basics (pg. 101) for binding instructions.

freestyle
churn dash

Most of you know that freestyle quilting isn't really my thing. It can be uncomfortable working without a pattern, not knowing what the final product might be. I'm all about measurements and exactness. I like to follow a pattern, knowing that I'm going to end up with perfectly finished blocks in an orderly quilt.

Freestyle quilts are different. Artistic decisions have to be made, and you're the one who has to make them. Eeek! But every once in awhile, I like to push myself creatively and stretch my brain. It's refreshing to leave the safety of my quilting comfort zone and sew something completely out-of-the-box. You have to let loose a little, and that can be scary, but once you get into the swing of things, it really is invigorating! It's healthy to expand your horizons, even if you feel a few growing pains in the process.

For the tutorial and everything you need to make this quilt visit:

www.msqc.co/blockearlywinter16

Many years ago, I decided I wanted to run. More specifically, I wanted to become a runner. You know the type, those gals in neon spandex that can jog for miles without breaking a sweat. But at the time my abilities were more along the lines of running a few hundred yards and stopping to catch my breath. It was a struggle.

It wasn't that I was too lazy for running; I was a pretty active person, but a brisk morning walk or a hike through the mountains just seemed to fit my body more comfortably than the jolting rhythm of a run. Still, I was determined.

I started slow with a bit of walking and jogging, then I'd break into short spurts of full-on running. After several months, I had worked myself up to one mile. A whole mile! I was so proud of myself! Even then, I just didn't enjoy it. Every step was labored, and I counted each lap around the track with desperation. You can do it! You can do it! You won't die! You're halfway there! I would think to myself. There were moments when I felt like a wild stallion, but other moments when I hit a brick wall.

Even though I never embraced running, I proved to myself that I could do it. I tried something new, and I had succeeded! I encourage each of you to step outside of your comfort zone and give something new a go. You just never know what you are capable of until you try!

materials

makes a 64" X 77½" quilt

QUILT TOP
- (1) package 10" print squares
- 3½ yards background

BORDER
- 1¼ yards

BINDING
- ¾ yard

BACKING
- 4¾ yards - vertical seam(s)

SAMPLE QUILT
- **Restful Raindrops** By Kathy Engle for Island Batiks

1 cut

From the background fabric, cut:

- (23) 5" strips across the width of the fabric – Subcut the strips into 5" squares for a **total of 180.**

Cut each of the 10" print squares in half to make (84) 5" x 10" rectangles.

2 sew unit A

Place the end of a print rectangle onto a 5" square with right sides facing at an angle – any angle will do! Stitch in place.

2A

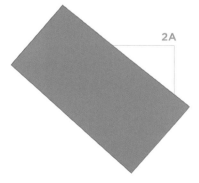

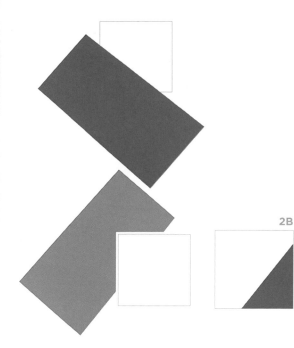

Press the sewn piece over the seam allowance. Turn the piece over and trim the excess fabric away evenly with the 5″ square. Reserve the rest of the print piece for another unit. There should be plenty of fabric left over to make at least one more. It's okay to leave the white fabric behind the print. **Make 4** Unit As per block. A **total of 80 Unit As** are needed to make the layout shown. 2B

3 sew unit b

Place a print rectangle over one side of a 5″ square, with right sides facing, at an angle. Be sure the angle covers the end of the square when it is flipped down and pressed. Sew in place and turn the piece over and trim the excess fabric away evenly with the 5″ square. Press. Again, reserve the rest of the print piece for another unit. **Make 4** per block. A **total of 80 Unit Bs** are needed to make the layout shown. 3A

4 block construction

Sew a Unit A to either side of a Unit B. Make 2 rows like this. 4A

Sew a Unit B to either side of a background 5″ square. Make 1 row like this. 4B

Sew the 3 rows together to complete the block. **Make 20.** 4C

Block Size: 13½″ Finished

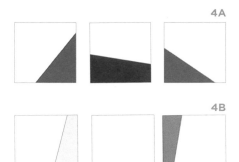

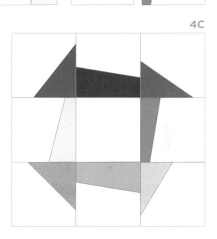

5 lay out blocks

Lay out the blocks in **5 rows** with each row having **4 blocks** across. When you are happy with the arrangement, sew the blocks into rows. Press the odd numbered rows toward the right and the even numbered rows toward the left. This will help the seams nest and make it easier to match up the corners.

Sew the rows together.

1   To make Unit A, place the end of a print rectangle onto a 5″ square with right sides facing at an angle. Stitch in place.

2   Turn the piece over and trim the excess fabric away evenly with the 5″ square to complete each Unit A.

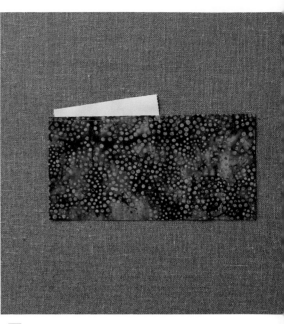

3   To make Unit B, place the end of a print rectangle onto a 5″ square with right sides facing. Notice that the angle is not as sharp as that used in Unit A. Stitch in place.

4   Press the sewn piece over the seam allowance and trim evenly with the edge of the 5″ square to complete the unit.

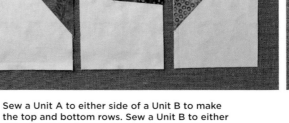

5   Sew a Unit A to either side of a Unit B to make the top and bottom rows. Sew a Unit B to either side of a 5″ background square to make the center row.

6   After all the rows are sewn together, press the completed block.

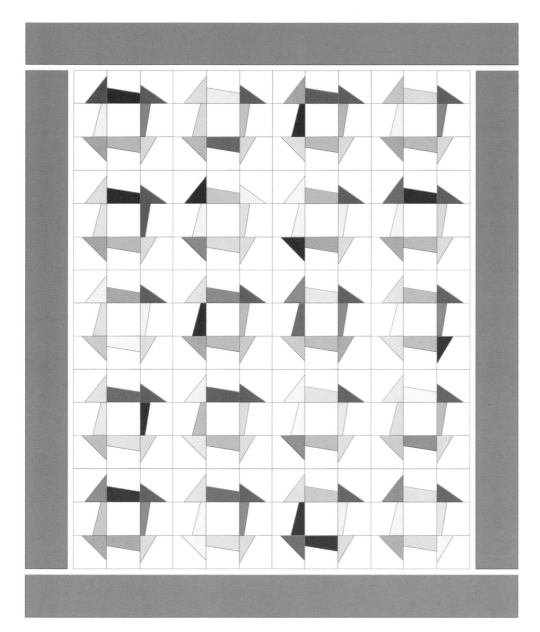

6 border

Cut (7) 5½" strips across the width of the fabric. Sew the strips together end-to-end to make one long strip. Trim the borders from this strip.

Refer to Borders (pg. 100) in the Construction Basics to measure and cut the outer borders. The strips are approximately 68" for the sides and approximately 64½" for the top and bottom.

7 quilt and bind

Layer the quilt with batting and backing and quilt. After the quilting is complete, square up the quilt and trim away all excess batting and backing. Add binding to complete the quilt. See Construction Basics (pg. 101) for binding instructions.

For the tutorial and everything you need to make this quilt visit:

www.msqc.co/blockearlywinter16

inside out

The other day my granddaughter came over all excited because she'd learned a new clapping game at school. As I watched her I said, "I used to do that all the time when I was a kid." She gave me a sidelong look that basically meant "Yeah right, Grandma," and so I did the only thing I could do. I pulled out the old clapping routine I had done so many times in grade school that now it's muscle memory. You probably remember the one: clap your hands together, clap left, clap right, then clap both hands with your partner. There was a clever little song that went along with it too, which I recited from memory. I was so good at those games when I was a little girl. My granddaughter was stunned and asked, "How did you know that?" As if she and her classmates were the first ones in the history of schoolyards to ever play a clapping game!

I think about all the games we played as kids and how eventually they all come back around. Do you remember those schoolyard rhymes for choosing who would be "it"? From

" I think about all the games we played as kids and how eventually they all come back around ... It makes me smile to remember all those silly things ... "

"Eeny, meeny, miny, mo" to "bubble gum, bubble gum in a dish" and the ever popular "ink-a-bink, a bottle of ink," they keep getting passed on through the generations. It makes me smile to remember all those silly things, and you know, I still sometimes hear my grandkids reciting them as they play together.

Ever since I wowed my granddaughter with my clapping game knowledge, I've been thinking of teaching her something else old that she'll think is brand new. Do you remember Cat's Cradle? I used to wear a string around my neck so that anytime someone wanted to play I'd be ready. Maybe I'll show my granddaughter a few of those good old string games. I bet she'll think they're the hottest new thing!

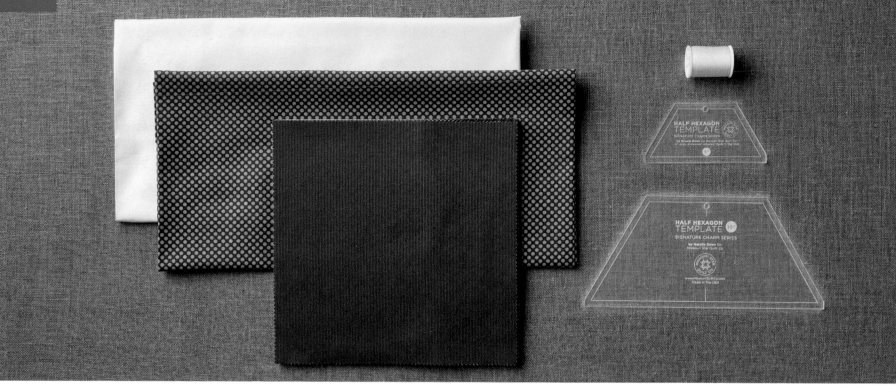

materials

makes a 65" x 65½" quilt

QUILT TOP
- 1 package of print 10" squares
- 1 package of background 10" squares
- 1 yard background fabric – includes top and bottom narrow border

OUTER BORDER
- 1 yard

BINDING
- ¾ yard

BACKING
- 4 yards - vertical seam(s)

OTHER SUPPLIES
- 5" MSQC Half-Hexagon Template
- 10" MSQC Half-Hexagon Template
- Lapel Glue Stick

SAMPLE QUILT
- **Dots and Stripes** for RJR Fabrics

1 cut

From the background fabric, cut:

- (4) 4⅝" strips across the width of the fabric – Subcut the strips into 20 half-hexagon shapes using the 10" Half-Hexagon Template. Each strip will yield 5 pieces if you flip the template 180 degrees each time you cut. You need a **total of 20.**

- Subcut 13 of the half-hexagon shapes into quarter hexagons by cutting them in half vertically. This will give you the correct pieces to fill in at the end of each row on both sides. Set aside the remaining 7 half-hexagons to use when sewing the rows together.

Set aside the remaining yardage for border strips at the top and bottom of the quilt.

2 pair and cut

Pair a 10" background square with a print 10" square. Cut the two squares in half thus creating 5" x 10" rectangles. Keep the two pairs together. Repeat for the remaining squares. **2A**

2A

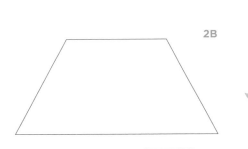
2B

3A

3B

From each set of 4 rectangles, cut:
- 1 large print half-hexagon using the 10″ MSQC Half-Hexagon Template

- 1 large background half-hexagon using the 10″ MSQC Half-Hexagon Template

- 1 small print half-hexagon using the 5″ MSQC Half-Hexagon Template **2B**

- 1 small background half-hexagon using the 5″ MSQC Half-Hexagon Template **2B**

NOTE: *When cutting the small half-hexagons, place the long edge of the template on the pinked edge of the rectangle. If you like, you can cut the pair of rectangles you are using for the small half-hexagons into 5″ squares and use half of them for another project.*

3 appliqué
Fold each large and small half-hexagon in half. Using your fingers, press the crease in place, this will help you place and align each piece.

Use the lapel glue stick to put a few dots or a swipe or two on the reverse side of a small print half-hexagon. Align the center creases of the two pieces. Press the sticky side of the small half-hexagon onto the right side of the large background half-hexagon. Using a small zigzag or buttonhole stitch, sew around the small half-hexagon to secure it in place. Leave the bottom of the piece unsewn as that edge will be caught in the seam allowance. **3A**

Repeat, this time using a small background half-hexagon atop a large print half-hexagon. Remember to keep the matching prints together! **3B**

Make **42 sets** of two rectangle blocks.

4 lay out blocks
Lay out your blocks in **13 rows** with each row having **7 blocks.** In the top and bottom rows, you will need to fill in with background half-hexagons. As you lay out the blocks, make sure the matching prints are placed together. Each row will begin and end with a large background quarter-hexagon. **4A**

When you are happy with the layout, sew the rows together.

4A

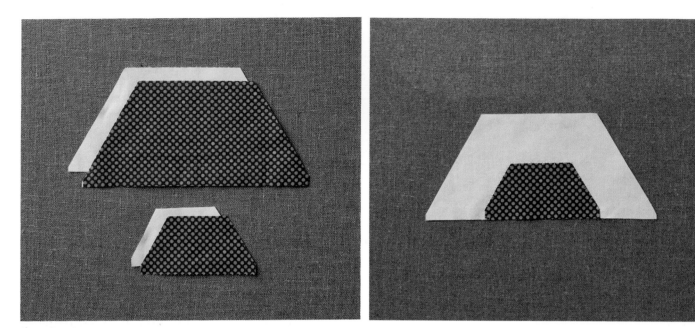

1 Using the MSQC templates, cut 1 large print and 1 large background half-hexagon. Cut 1 small print and 1 small background half-hexagon. Keep all pieces using the same prints together.

2 Appliqué a small half-hexagon to a large background half-hexagon using a small zigzag or buttonhole stitch.

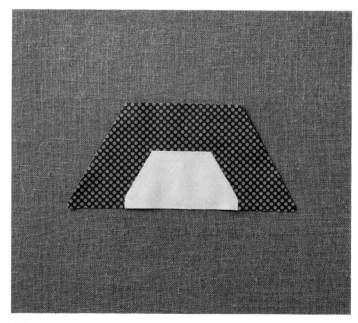

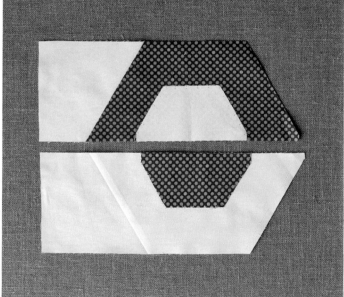

3 Appliqué a small background half-hexagon to a large print half-hexagon using a small zigzag or buttonhole stitch.

4 Lay out the rows, making sure the matching prints are placed together. Each row will begin and end with a large background quarter-hexagon.

5 top and bottom borders

From the remaining background yardage, cut (4) 2½" strips across the width of the fabric. Sew 2 strips together and trim to approximately 57½". Make 2 and sew one to the top and one to the bottom of the quilt. Refer to page 100 in the Construction Basics for measuring and cutting instructions.

6 outer border

From the outer border fabric, cut:

- (7) 4½" strips across the width of the fabric. Sew the strips together end-to-end to make one long strip. Trim the borders from this strip.

Refer to Borders (pg. 100) in the Construction Basics to measure and cut the inner borders. The strips are approximately 58⅛" for the sides and approximately 65½" for the top and bottom.

7 quilt and bind

Layer the quilt with batting and backing and quilt. After the quilting is complete, square up the quilt and trim away all excess batting and backing. Add binding to complete the quilt. See Construction Basics (pg. 101) for binding instructions.

*For the tutorial and everything
you need to make this quilt visit:*

www.msqc.co/blockearlywinter16

summer
nights

One day a friendly quilter came into my shop to stock up on supplies. While we were chatting, she casually mentioned that she was saving a one-inch square of every fabric she had ever used. Her plan was to eventually stitch them together into a postage stamp quilt. I looked at her in amazement and smiled saying, "Wow! I am so happy for you!" Of course, in my mind I was really thinking, are you crazy? Do you realize what you are undertaking? That's a project I'd never finish in a lifetime!

Just imagine sewing a quarter-inch seam all the way around an itty-bitty one-inch square. That one inch instantly shrinks down to a half-inch or less. Even if she has thousands of squares, that is going to be one tiny quilt—a beautiful quilt to be sure, but an incredibly difficult one to piece together.

I do love postage stamp quilts, I just don't have the patience for all those single squares! When you lay out a quilt using single squares, it takes forever to get all the colors nicely dispersed. Then, when you sew your rows together and put them back into the quilt, chances are you'll have two yellows that line up and stick out like a sore thumb. Assuming you accidentally flipped a row, you turn it upside down, only to discover that not only do two different yellow squares now touch, but you've got a whole clump of red hanging out together on one side. So you take that row out and shift it to the top of the quilt, and that's when things get crazy! Nothing looks right anymore! Soon you've got the husband involved and you're swapping rows and pulling out your hair and cursing yourself for ever starting such an infuriating project!

This, my friends, is the reason I've developed my "quick and easy" methods. I just think piecing should be simpler! I want you to enjoy every step of quilt creation, so I try to make the whole process as frustration-free as possible. For example, this Summer Nights quilt is constructed with 4-patches, not single squares. If two colors line up, simply rotate that 4-patch. Easy peasy! I hope you enjoy this simplified way of making a postage stamp table topper. The result is bound to be lovely, and no one will ever know how easy it was to put together!

materials

makes a 34" X 34" quilt

TABLE TOPPER TOP
• 1 package 5" print squares

INNER BORDER
• ¼ yard

OUTER BORDER
• ¾ yard

BINDING
• ½ yard

BACKING
• 1¼ yards

OTHER SUPPLIES
• Scallops Vines & Waves Template by Quilt in a Day (optional)
• The Bias Ruler by TQM (optional)

SAMPLE QUILT
• **Belcourt** by Studio RK for Robert Kaufman Fabrics

1 sew

Layer 2 print squares together with right sides facing. Join the two by sewing along 2 opposite edges using a ¼" seam allowance. **Make 18. 1A**

Cut each sewn set of squares in half between the seams at 2½".

NOTE: *We are measuring from the outside edge of the squares rather than from the sewn seam! Open to reveal 2 charm units. Press the seam allowances toward the darker fabric.* **Make 36. 1B**

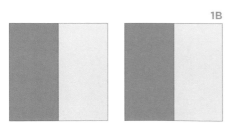

1A

1B

1C

1D

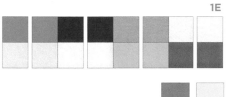
1E

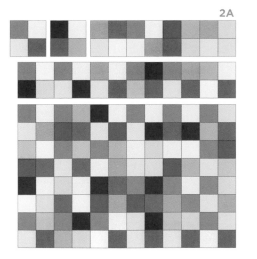
2A

Sew the charm units together end-to-end to make a long, pieced strip. **1C**

Cut one 2½″ wide piece from the first charm unit and set aside for the moment. **1D**

Fold the remaining half of the first charm unit over the next charm unit in the pieced strip. The right sides will be facing. Cut along the edge of the previously cut piece to make a 4-patch unit. Repeat, folding and cutting until you reach the end of the strip. You will have (1) 2-patch piece left at the end. Sew it to the first piece you trimmed off at the beginning. You will end up with **(36) 4-patch blocks. 1E**

2 lay out and sew

Arrange the 4-patch blocks in **6 rows** with each row having **6 blocks**. Sew each row together. Press the seam allowances of the odd numbered rows toward the right and the even numbered rows toward the left. This will make the seams nest and make it easier to match up the blocks. **2A**

3 inner border

Cut (3) 1½″ strips across the width of the fabric. Sew the strips together end-to-end to make one long strip. Trim the borders from this strip.

Refer to Borders (pg. 100) in the Construction Basics to measure and cut the inner borders. The strips are approximately 24½″ for the sides and approximately 26½″ for the top and bottom.

4 outer border

Cut (4) 4½″ strips across the width of the fabric. Sew the strips together end-to-end to make one long strip. Trim the borders from this strip.

Refer to Borders (pg. 100) in the Construction Basics to measure and cut the outer borders. The strips are approximately 26½″ for the sides and approximately 34½″ for the top and bottom.

Using the Scallops, Vines & Waves ruler, follow the manufacturer's instructions and mark the scallops on the border. Do not cut the scallops until the quilt has been quilted!

5 quilt and bind

Layer the quilt with batting and backing and quilt. After the quilting is complete, cut the marked scallops, thus trimming away all excess batting and backing. Add binding to complete the quilt. See Construction Basics (pg. 101) for binding instructions.

1 Layer 2 print squares together with right sides facing. Join the two by sewing along 2 opposite edges using a ¼" seam allowance. Cut each sewn set of square in half between the seams.

2 Open to reveal 2 charm units. Press the seam allowances toward the darker fabric.

3 Sew the charm units together end-to-end to make a long, piece strip.

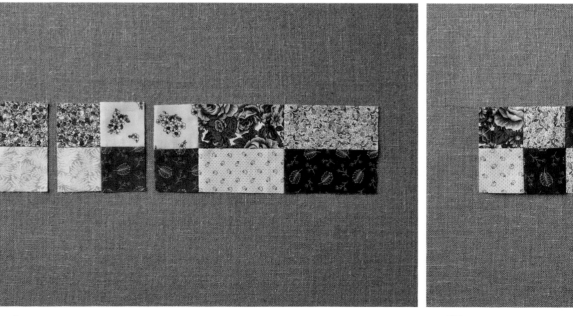

4 Cut (1) 2½" wide piece from the first charm unit and set aside for the moment. Fold the remaining half of the first charm unit over the next charm unit in the strip and cut along the edge to make a 4-patch.

5 Sew the 4-patches together to make each row.

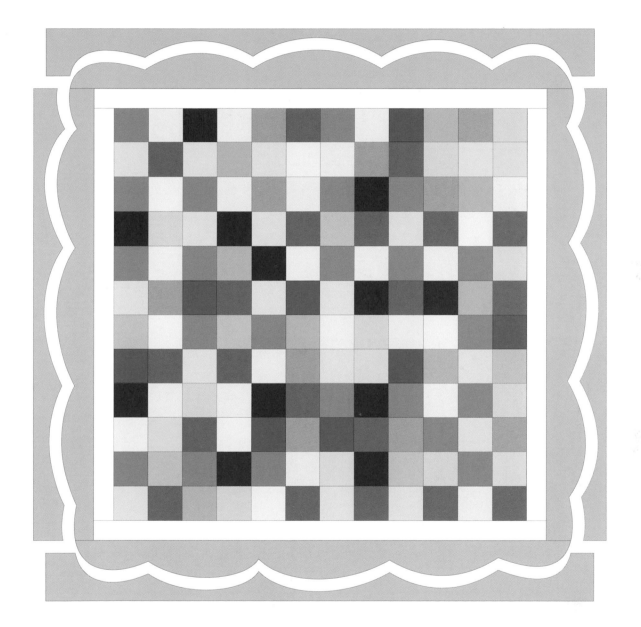

For the tutorial and everything you need to make this quilt visit:
www.msqc.co/blockearlywinter16

sweet petunia

I spent much of my young life performing in the theatre. There's nothing quite like being up on stage! When I started having children, I didn't want to give up that part of myself, so I was determined to participate in as many shows as I could. It worked out okay at first, but my schedule was crazy, and sometimes I would have to bring my children along with me. I started to worry that my little noisemakers and I would be asked to leave and never come back, so I made myself indispensable. I offered to sew costumes for the theatre group so they would need me to stay, kids and all!

I had been sewing clothing for years, but I quickly discovered that costuming is an entirely different art. When constructing clothes, I did everything I could to make my pieces look flawlessly professional. Costumes, on the other hand, only have to look good from twenty feet away. They

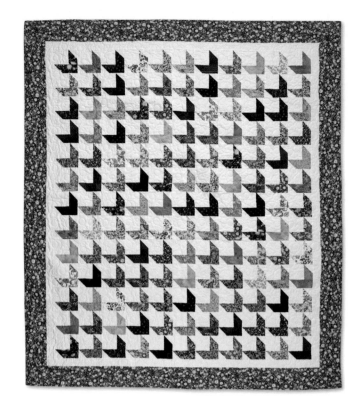

don't need French seams or satin linings. Goodness sakes, they only have to last the two-week run of the production! And if something goes wrong, it's certainly nothing a safety pin or two can't handle. Then again, costumes do need to be more bold. Bright colors, sparkling sequins, and explosions of ruffles—the sky was the limit, and my imagination went wild!

Making costumes filled the part of me that craves a creative outlet. I was a happier person, and I was a better, more fun mom. I realized that I was capable of making just about any costume my kids could ever want. When Halloween rolled around, I was like a fairy godmother, cranking out knights, ninjas, vampires, and queens that were the envy of the entire neighborhood. We still have bins of costumes, and nothing brings me more pleasure than having the grandkids over to dig for treasures.

Last year, a couple of my granddaughters participated in their school's production of Alice in Wonderland. Of course, their first stop was my house to find costumes. "Grandma, do you have a rabbit costume?" "How about a funny hat?" "I need a duchess outfit. Do you have any ideas?" And just like that, I became magic to them again, and it filled me up with creative energy like it did so many years ago.

If you can sew, never underestimate what a gift that is! You are not just a quilter, a tailor, or a seamstress. You are a maker, and you have the power to bring dreams to life!

materials

makes a 74½" X 85½" quilt

QUILT TOP
- 1 roll 2½" strips
- 3½ yards background – includes inner border

OUTER BORDER
- 1½ yards

BINDING
- ¾ yard

BACKING
- 5¼ yards - vertical seam(s)

SAMPLE QUILT
- **Regent Street Lawns** by Sentimental Studios for Moda Fabrics

1 sew

From each of the print strips, cut:

- (4) 2½" x 6" rectangles
- (4) 2½" x 4" rectangles

Stack all pieces cut from the same strip together. Pair the 6" rectangles and the 4" rectangles of the same print together.

From the background fabric, cut:

- (15) 4" strips across the width of the fabric – Subcut the strips into 4" squares for a **total of 143 squares.**

- (25) 2½" strips across the width of the fabric – Subcut 18 of the strips into 2½" squares. Each strip will yield (16) squares and you need a **total of 286.**

Set aside the remaining 7 strips to use for the inner border.

2 sew

For each block, fold (2) 2½" squares once on the diagonal. Press the crease in place to mark your sewing line. **2A**

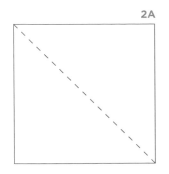

2A

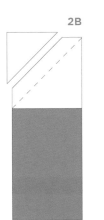

2B

2C

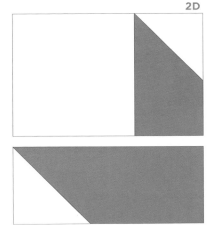

2D

Select a pair of matching rectangles. Place a 2½" creased background square on 1 end of a 2½" x 6" rectangle with right sides facing as shown. (Notice the angle the square is sewn onto the rectangle.) Sew on the crease, then trim ¼" away from the sewn seam. Open and press the seam allowance toward the print. **2B**

Place a 2½" square on 1 end of the 2½" x 4" rectangles with right sides facing as shown. (Notice the angle of the square is opposite of that you stitched onto the 6" rectangles.) Sew on the crease, then trim ¼" away from the sewn seam. Open and press the seam allowance toward the print.
Make 4. 2C

Sew a short rectangle to a 4" background square. Add a long rectangle as shown to complete the block. **Make 143. 2D**

Block Size: 5½" finished

3 arrange

Lay out the blocks in 13 rows with each row made up of 11 blocks. When you are happy with the arrangement, sew the blocks together. Press the seam allowances of the odd numbered rows toward the right and the even numbered rows toward the left. This will make the seams nest, making it easier to match up the corners of the blocks.

4 inner border

Sew the (7) 2½" background strips you set aside earlier together end-to-end to make one long strip. Trim the borders from this strip.

Refer to Borders (pg. 100) in the Construction Basics to measure and cut the inner borders. The strips are approximately 72" for the sides and approximately 65" for the top and bottom.

5 outer border

Cut (8) 5½" strips across the width of the fabric. Sew the strips together end-to-end to make one long strip. Trim the borders from this strip.

Refer to Borders (pg. 100) in the Construction Basics to measure and cut the outer borders. The strips are approximately 76" for the sides and approximately 75" for the top and bottom.

6 quilt and bind

Layer the quilt with batting and backing and quilt. After the quilting is complete, square up the quilt and trim away all excess batting and backing. Add binding to complete the quilt. See Construction Basics (pg. 101) for binding instructions.

1 Place a marked 2½″ background square atop a 6″ rectangle with right sides facing. Sew on the marked line, then trim ¼″ away from the sewn seam. Note the direction of the angle.

2 Place a marked 2½″ background square atop a 4″ rectangle with right sides facing. Sew on the marked line, then trim ¼″ away from the sewn seam. Notice the direction of the angle.

3 Sew a short rectangle to a 4″ background square as shown.

4 Add a long rectangle as shown to complete the block.

5 Arrange and sew the blocks together into rows.

For the tutorial and everything you need to make this quilt visit: **www.msqc.co/blockearlywinter16**

tea party

As I have traveled around the world teaching, many of you have gotten to know my darling husband, Ron. He is a gem, or as some would say, a keeper. I've been asked about our love story so many times that I decided it's time to share it.

You may be surprised to learn that when Ron and I started dating, I had a fourteen-month-old baby and was quite pregnant with my second child. We had actually met years earlier, but Ron had left the area for two years to serve a mission for our church, and I had fallen in love, married, and started a family. When my marriage ended, I found myself alone, living with my parents, and wondering where my path would lead. That was just about the time that Ron re-entered the picture. One Sunday morning, I ran into him at church. He was so excited to see me, and glad to find out I was single. We began to date, and we had so much fun together.

Years ago, we had met at a church dance. I'm four years younger than him and I was all garbed out in my hippy gear and he looked like one of the Bee Gees. Initially, he was very shy and during the short time we talked and danced, he fell madly in love with me, although I had no idea. We didn't actually get together until four years later.

When I first met Ron, he was too shy to say much to me, but things changed after he came home from his mission. He spoke a lot more—in full sentences! Then one day he came over to fix my car and never really left. He just kept coming over every day from then on. We would sit and talk on the couch, I would sit on one end and he'd be on the other. We just talked and got to be really, really good friends.

He was nice. Really nice. And I wasn't used to that. Because of my previous relationship, I had a hard time trusting his words and intentions, so when he asked me to marry him, I was unsure. Why would he want to be with someone like me? Did I really want someone like him? I did love him, but not with that fiery passion you see in the movies. I knew he would make a good husband and father, but I was afraid of making another mistake.

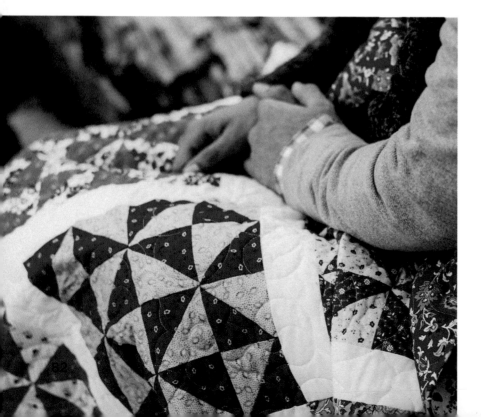

I shared all my doubts and concerns with Ron and waited for him to turn around and leave, but he didn't. He knelt down in front of me, took my hands in his, and said, "I will love you so much, you will learn to love me." I knew he meant it, so I said yes. And he was right. That love came so fast, and it has never stopped growing since.

I am thankful everyday for this wonderful man of mine. Over the years, our love has grown and blossomed. We have now been married for 36 years, and I have never been happier!

materials

makes a 68" X 80½" quilt

QUILT TOP
- (1) package 10" print squares
- 1½ yards background fabric – includes inner border

OUTER BORDER
- 1¾ yards

BINDING
- ¾ yard

BACKING
- 5 yards - vertical seam(s)

SAMPLE QUILT
- **Garnett** by Nancy Zieman for for Penny Rose Fabrics

1 cut

Separate the 10" squares into 2 stacks, one dark and one light. Some of your prints may fall into the medium category and you will have to decide whether you call them "light" or "dark." Don't get overly concerned about this because as long as they are paired with a contrasting color, they will work.

From each of the 10" print squares, cut:

- (4) 5" squares. Stack the matching prints together.

From the background fabric, cut:

- (14) 2½" x width of fabric strips – subcut 7 of the strips into (3) 2½" x 11" rectangles for a **total of 20.** We'll call these pieces rectangle A for the sake of clarity. Subcut the remaining 7 strips into (3) 2½" x 13" rectangles for a **total of 20.** We'll call these pieces rectangle B. Set aside the rest of the fabric for the inner border.

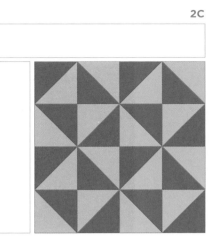

2A

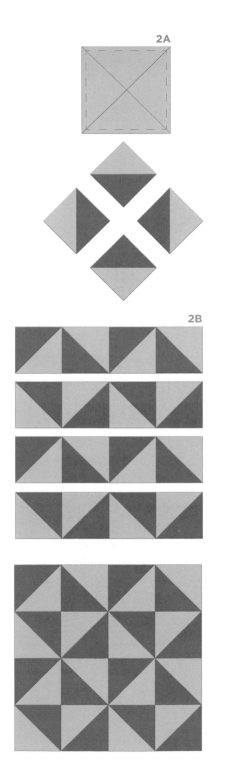

2B

2C

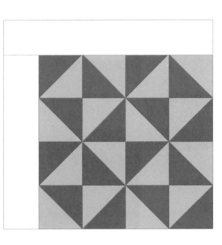

Repeat and make 3 more sets of 4 matching half-square triangle units. You should have a **total of 16** matching half-square triangles.

Lay out the matching half-square triangles into 4 rows of 4 as shown. Sew the rows together to complete the block. **2B**

Repeat and make a total of **20 blocks.**

Block Size: 10½" Finished

To each block, add a background rectangle A to the left side and a rectangle B to the top. **2C**

3 lay out blocks

Lay out the blocks in **5 rows** with each row having **4 blocks.** Notice that every other block in the row is flipped 180 degrees.

2 sew unit A

Choose 4 matching light print squares and 4 matching dark print squares.

Place a light print square atop a dark print square and sew all the way around the perimeter using a ¼" seam allowance. Cut each square from corner to corner twice on the diagonal. Open to reveal 1 set of 4 half-square triangle units, and press the seam allowances toward the darker fabric. **2A**

4 inner border

Cut (6) 2½" strips across the width of the fabric. Sew the strips together end-to-end to make one long strip. Trim the borders from this strip.

Refer to Borders (pg. 100) in the Construction Basics to measure and cut the inner borders. The strips are approximately 63" for the sides and approximately 54½" for the top and bottom.

1 Layer a light print square with a darker print square with right sides facing. Sew all the way around the perimeter using a ¼" seam allowance.

2 Cut the sewn square from corner to corner twice on the diagonal. Open and press the seam allowance toward the darker fabric.

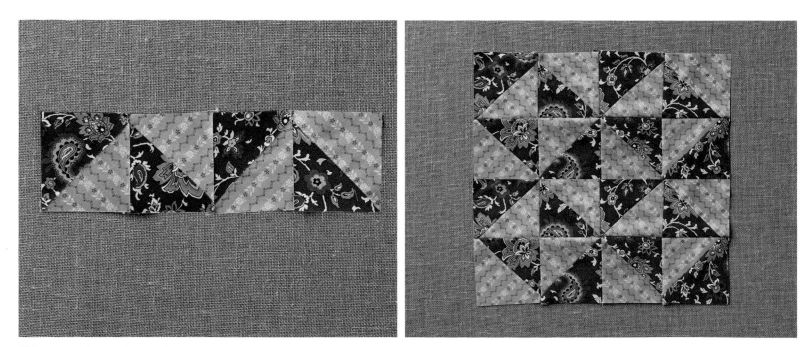

3 Lay out the matching half-square triangles into 4 rows of 4 units. See the diagram for the block on page 85.

4 Sew the 4 rows together to complete the block.

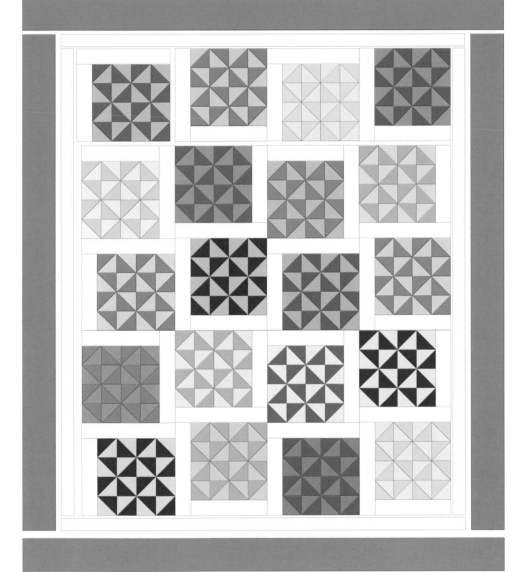

5 outer border

Cut (8) 7½" strips across the width of the fabric. Sew the strips together end-to-end to make one long strip. Trim the borders from this strip.

Refer to Borders (pg. 100) in the Construction Basics to measure and cut the outer borders. The strips are approximately 67" for the sides and approximately 68½" for the top and bottom.

6 quilt and bind

Layer the quilt with batting and backing and quilt. After the quilting is complete, square up the quilt and trim away all excess batting and backing. Add binding to complete the quilt. See Construction Basics (pg. 101) for binding instructions.

color yourself quilty

In our hectic world it's nice to take a break and get back to basics. Maybe that's why the adult coloring craze has taken off in such a big way! It's a reminder of the simple pleasures in life. When my children were little, I would often plunk down right next to them, grab a coloring book, and fill in those pages with my trusty box of crayons. It always soothed my nerves and gave my mind a place to go, instead of worrying about the stacks of dishes waiting for me or the pile of laundry on the couch. So I wasn't surprised when, not too long ago, coloring books for grown-ups started popping up everywhere. I could have used one 25 years ago!

Here at Missouri Star, we figured it was about time we joined in the fun and made our own coloring book. This beautiful new book has been designed especially for quilters. With patterns that bring peace of mind, it's a great way to plan quilts, explore new possibilities, or just unwind with some of your favorite designs. You'll find quilts pulled right from the pages of Block, so it makes a great compliment to the magazine. Experiment with color and if you make a little mistake, there are no seams to rip! Go ahead and pull out your crayons, colored pencils, or markers and take some time to unwind with us.

Try it out! We've provided some coloring book options taken from this issue to fill in and explore your very own color versions of these blocks.

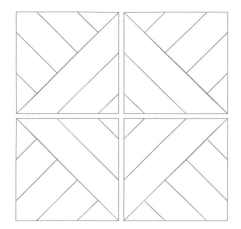
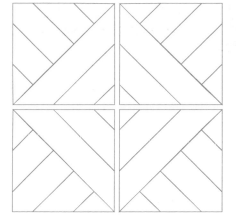
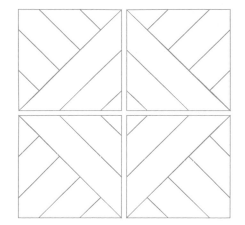

desert sunset blocks

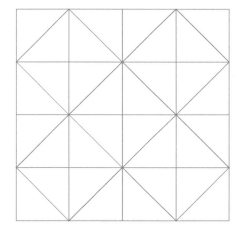
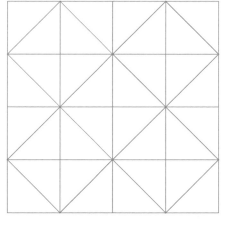
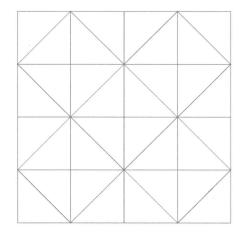

tea party blocks

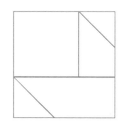
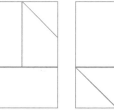
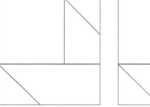

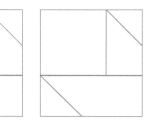

sweet petunia blocks

baby kisses

QUILT SIZE
51" X 51"

QUILT TOP
2 packages 5" squares
1¾ yards background fabric -
  includes inner border

OUTER BORDER
¾ yard

BINDING
½ yard

BACKING
3¼ yards - vertical seam(s)

SAMPLE QUILT
Garden Girl by Zoe Pearn for Riley
  Blake Designs

ONLINE TUTORIALS
msqc.co/blockearlywinter16

QUILTING
Flutterby

PATTERN
pg. 8

butterfly blossoms

QUILT SIZE
56" X 66"

QUILT TOP
2 packages 5" print squares
2 packages 5" background squares
¾ yard background – includes sashing
   strips and inner border.

OUTER BORDER
1½ yards

BINDING
¾ yard

BACKING
3¾ yards - horizontal seam(s)

OTHER SUPPLIES
MSQC Periwinkle Template

OPTIONAL
Glue Stick – We use Lapel Sticks

SAMPLE QUILT
Daisy Blue by Flaurie & Finch
   for RJR Fabrics

ONLINE TUTORIALS
msqc.co/blockearlywinter16

QUILTING
Little Nature

PATTERN
pg. 16

desert
sunset

QUILT SIZE
59" X 59"

QUILT TOP
1 roll of 2½" x 42" strips

OUTER BORDER
¾ yards

BINDING
¾ yard

BACKING
3¾ yards - vertical seam(s)

SAMPLE QUILT
Katie's Cupboard by Kim Diehl
    for Henry Glass

ONLINE TUTORIALS
msqc.co/blockearlywinter16

QUILTING
Loops & Swirls

PATTERN
pg. 24

diamond dash

QUILT SIZE
77" X 81"

QUILT TOP
1 package (42 ct.) 10" squares

SNOWBALLED CORNERS, SASHING
STRIPS, & INNER BORDER
1¾ yards solid fabric

OUTER BORDER
1½ yards

BINDING
¾ yard

BACKING
5 yards - vertical seam(s)

SAMPLE QUILT
Vine for Windham Fabrics by
    The Henry Ford Collection

ONLINE TUTORIALS
msqc.co/blockearlywinter16

QUILTING
Cotton Candy

PATTERN
pg. 36

flirty

TABLE RUNNER SIZE
42" X 16"

TABLE RUNNER TOP
(12) 5" squares
1/2 yard background

BORDER AND BINDING
¾ yard

BACKING
¾ yards

SAMPLE QUILT
Paintbox Solids by Elizabeth
   Hartman for Robert Kaufman

ONLINE TUTORIALS
msqc.co/blockearlywinter16

QUILTING
Large Hearts

PATTERN
pg. 40

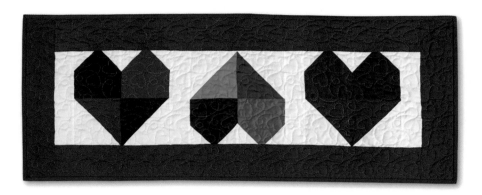

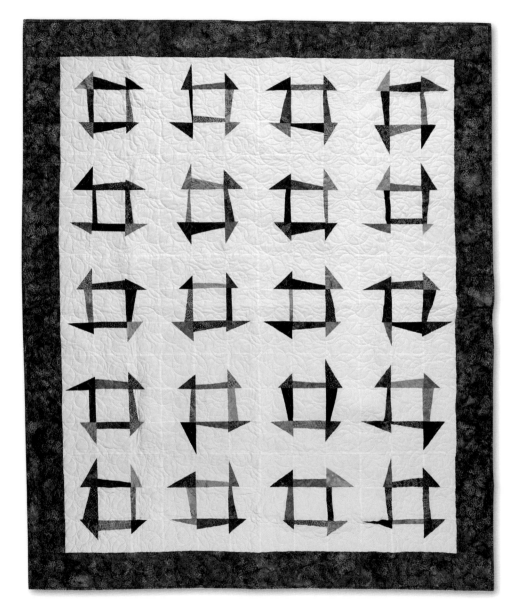

freestyle
churn dash

QUILT SIZE
64" X 77½"

QUILT TOP
(1) package 10" print squares
3½ yards background

BORDER
1¼ yards

BINDING
¾ yard

BACKING
4¾ yards - vertical seams

SAMPLE QUILT
Restful Raindrops By Kathy Engle
 for Island Batiks

ONLINE TUTORIALS
msqc.co/blockearlywinter16

QUILTING
Arc Doodle

QUILT PATTERN
pg. 48

inside out

QUILT SIZE
65" X 65½"

QUILT TOP
1 package of print 10" squares
1 package of background 10" squares
1 yard background fabric – includes top
    and bottom narrow border

OUTER BORDER
1 yard

BINDING
¾ yard

BACKING
4 yards - vertical seam(s)

OTHER SUPPLIES
5" MSQC Half-Hexagon Template
10" MSQC Half-Hexagon Template
Lapel Glue Stick

SAMPLE QUILT
Dots and Stripes by RJR Fabrics

ONLINE TUTORIALS
msqc.co/blockearlywinter16

QUILTING
Cotton Candy

QUILT PATTERN
pg. 56

summer nights

TABLE TOPPER SIZE
34" X 34"

TABLE TOPPER TOP
1 package 5" print squares

INNER BORDER
¼ yard

OUTER BORDER
¾ yard

BINDING
½ yard

BACKING
1¼ yards

OTHER SUPPLIES
Scallops Vines & Waves Template
   by Quilt in a Day (optional)
The Bias Ruler by TQM (optional)

SAMPLE QUILT
Belcourt by Studio RK for
   Robert Kaufman Fabrics

ONLINE TUTORIALS
msqc.co/blockearlywinter16

QUILTING
Faster Posies

PATTERN
pg. 64

sweet petunia

QUILT SIZE
74½" X 85½"

QUILT TOP
1 roll 2½" strips
3½ yards background – includes
    inner border

OUTER BORDER
1½ yards

BINDING
¾ yard

BACKING
5¼ yards - vertical seam(s)

SAMPLE QUILT
Regent Street Lawns by
    Sentimental Studios for
    Moda Fabrics

ONLINE TUTORIALS
msqc.co/blockearlywinter16

QUILTING
Loops & Swirls

PATTERN
pg. 72

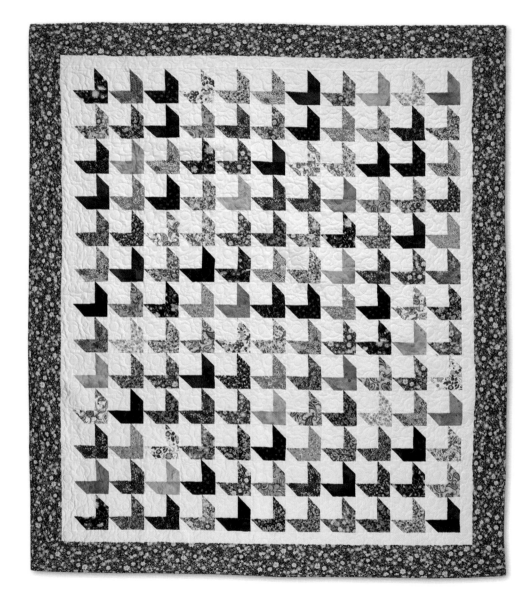

tea party

QUILT SIZE
68" X 80½"

QUILT TOP
1½ yards background fabric –
   includes inner border
(1) package 10" print squares

OUTER BORDER
1¾ yards

BINDING
¾ yard

BACKING
5 yards - vertical seam(s)

SAMPLE QUILT
Garnet by Nancy Zieman for
   Penny Rose Fabrics

ONLINE TUTORIALS
msqc.co/blockearlywinter16

QUILTING
Flower Swirls

PATTERN
pg. 80

construction basics

- All seams are ¼" inch unless directions specify differently.

- Cutting instructions are given at the point when cutting is required.

- Precuts are not prewashed; therefore do not prewash other fabrics in the project

- All strips are cut WOF

- Remove all selvages

ACRONYMS USED

MSQC	Missouri Star Quilt Co.
RST	right sides together
WST	wrong sides together
HST	half-square triangle
WOF	width of fabric
LOF	length of fabric

pre-cut glossary

5" SQUARE PACK

1 = (42) 5" squares or ¾ yd of fabric
1 = baby
2 = crib
3 = lap
4 = twin

2½" STRIP ROLL

1 = (40) 2½" strip roll cut the width of fabric
    or 2¾ yds of fabric
1 = a twin
2 = queen

10" SQUARE PACK

1 = (42) 10" square pack of fabric: 2¾ yds total
1 = a twin
2 = queen

When we mention a precut, we are basing the pattern on a 40-42 count pack. Not all precuts have the same count, so be sure to check the count on your precut to make sure you have enough pieces to complete your project.

general quilting
- All seams are ¼" inch unless directions specify differently.
- Cutting instructions are given at the point when cutting is required.
- Precuts are not prewashed; therefore do not prewash other fabrics in the project.
- All strips are cut width of fabric.
- Remove all selvages.

press seams
- Use the cotton setting on your iron when pressing.
- Press the seam just as it was sewn RST. This "sets" the seam.
- To set the seam, press just as it was sewn with right sides together.
- With dark fabric on top, lift the dark fabric and press back.
- The seam allowance is pressed toward the dark side. Some patterns may direct otherwise for certain situations.
- Press toward borders. Pieced borders may demand otherwise.
- Press diagonal seams open on binding to reduce bulk.

borders
- Always measure the quilt top 3 times before cutting borders.
- Start measuring about 4" in from each side and through the center vertically.
- Take the average of those 3 measurements.
- Cut 2 border strips to that size. Piece strips together if needed.
- Attach one to either side of the quilt.
- Position the border fabric on top as you sew. The feed dogs can act like rufflers. Having the border on top will prevent waviness and keep the quilt straight.
- Repeat this process for the top and bottom borders, measuring the width 3 times.
- Include the newly attached side borders in your measurements.
- Press toward the borders.

binding

find a video tutorial at: www.msqc.co/006

- Use 2½" strips for binding.
- Sew strips end-to-end into one long strip with diagonal seams, aka plus sign method (next). Press seams open.
- Fold in half lengthwise wrong sides together and press.
- The entire length should equal the outside dimension of the quilt plus 15" - 20."

plus sign method

- Lay one strip across the other as if to make a plus sign right sides together.
- Sew from top inside to bottom outside corners crossing the intersections of fabric as you sew. Trim excess to ¼" seam allowance.
- Press seam open.

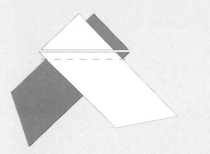

attach binding

- Match raw edges of folded binding to the quilt top edge.
- Leave a 10" tail at the beginning.
- Use a ¼" seam allowance.
- Start in the middle of a long straight side.

find a video tutorial at: www.msqc.co/001

10" tail   ¼"

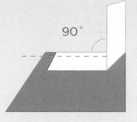

90°   fold

miter corners

- Stop sewing ¼" before the corner.
- Move the quilt out from under the presser foot.
- Clip the threads.
- Flip the binding up at a 90° angle to the edge just sewn.
- Fold the binding down along the next side to be sewn, aligning raw edges.
- The fold will lie along the edge just completed.
- Begin sewing on the fold.

close binding

*MSQC recommends **The Binding Tool** from TQM Products to finish binding perfectly every time.*

- Stop sewing when you have 12" left to reach the start.
- Where the binding tails come together, trim excess leaving only 2½" of overlap.
- It helps to pin or clip the quilt together at the two points where the binding starts and stops. This takes the pressure off of the binding tails while you work.
- Use the plus sign method to sew the two binding ends together, except this time when making the plus sign, match the edges. Using a pencil, mark your sewing line because you won't be able to see where the corners intersect. Sew across.

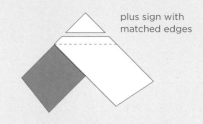

plus sign with
matched edges

- Trim off excess; press seam open.
- Fold in half wrong sides together, and align all raw edges to the quilt top.
- Sew this last binding section to the quilt. Press.
- Turn the folded edge of the binding around to the back of the quilt and tack into place with an invisible stitch or machine stitch if you wish.

THE FAIR THIEF

PART 5

Attack of the Drone

A JENNY DOAN MYSTERY

written by Steve Westover

It seemed like too much to hope that her trap could have already caught its prey, but MK watched as the balding man lurked around the trailer. He wore khaki shorts and a green polo shirt with the insignia of the state fair on the chest. MK judged by his pudgy midsection and receding hairline that he was in his forties, but as he stepped out of the trailer's shadow MK could see her first impression was wrong. A patchy beard tried desperately, but unsuccessfully to cover the man's twenty-five-year-old baby face. He ambled toward the trailer door as he looked at his phone.

"What is he up to?" MK asked herself. Safe in her seclusion on the other side of the clearing, she studied the man. She tapped a button on her phone. "Hey, Buck. Can you get a good picture of this guy? Like a close up of his face?"

MK could hear rustling on the other side of the phone and then she heard Buck whisper, "Yeah. Give me a second."

"Good. Text me an image," MK said. She settled against a green golf cart full of tools, shovels, and rakes, content to watch her subject when she flinched at a touch on her elbow. She spun around, her eyes wide with surprise.

"Whoa, there. Relax. It's just me," Jenny said. "I didn't mean to startle you."

MK's shoulders rose with a deep breath and then she forced a smile. She pointed to the man loitering near the trailer. "It looks like he works for the fair, but I can't be sure if he's up to something."

Jenny looked at the man and then leaned forward and squinted.

"Need some glasses?" MK quipped.

"Oh shush," Jenny scolded.

"Look up there," MK said. Jenny followed MK's gaze. Overhead, the drone maneuvered to a position directly in front of the man. Seconds later, MK's phone pinged. "Nice!" MK opened the text and then studied the attached image.

Jenny looked over MK's shoulder. Her eyebrows rose when she saw the face on the screen. "I know that guy."

MK couldn't hide her surprise. "Really? Do share." MK's phone pinged again. She opened another text from Buck that simply read "HELP!"

Jenny's and MK's eyes met briefly before they turned in unison toward the trailer. The man was gone. "Where'd he go?" Jenny asked anxiously. Not waiting for an answer, Jenny strode toward the trailer, her long legs carrying her quickly, making it difficult for MK to keep up.

MK texted Buck while she was walking. "We're coming. Hang on."

Jenny and MK slowed as they approached the trailer, listening carefully to the sounds coming from within. There were rustling sounds, then a moment of calm before a cacophony of crashes, clatters, and smashes breached the silence. Jenny's heart pounded in her chest and her jaw clenched. She felt the anger of a mama bear rise within her. She balled her fists to her tightened shoulders as she imagined the danger Buck was facing. Her face turned red with rage as she prepared to charge.

MK had only seen that expression once before and it had ended with Jenny ramming a suspected murderer with a hotel cleaning cart. She grabbed Jenny's arm, trying to hold her back, but Jenny shook it off. She bounded the final steps toward the door and reached for the knob, but the door opened and the balding man raced out. His arms were wrapped around a black electronic box that looked like a digital video recorder. He lowered his shoulder and brushed past Jenny, knocking her flat to the ground. MK stared into his crazy eyes as he rushed past. "Jenny!" MK screamed, reaching to help Jenny from the ground.

Jenny rose onto her hands and knees and then stood. Dirt covered her clothes, but she didn't take the time to dust off. "Check on Buck and call the police!" Jenny yelled as she started hobbling across the clearing in pursuit. Her first steps were unsure as her left knee twinged with sharp pain, but her stride lengthened and the pain seemed to disappear as she focused on the squatty man running from her. Still, the man's lead grew as he passed the clearing and turned down a side path behind a booth.

Jenny raced to the green golf cart and sat down. She turned the key, backed up, and raced in the direction the man had gone. She wiped the sweat from her brow as she searched for the man. She turned down another pathway, searching frantically, but she couldn't see him anywhere.

***

MK's eyes widened with horror as she stepped inside the trailer. The overturned desk leaned against two office chairs and computer monitors lay smashed on the floor. "Buck!" She yelled, "Where are you!?"

From the doorway leading into the back room, she saw Buck's head peek around the corner. He motioned with his head. "Come here."

MK stepped over the monitor and pushed aside a file cabinet that was leaning against a wall. It crashed to the floor. "Thank goodness," MK said as she reached Buck. She looked him in the eye. "You're okay?"

"He grabbed the DVR with the footage from last night," Buck said. "He thinks he has the evidence."

"But he doesn't," MK said. She smiled.

Buck also grinned. "No, he doesn't." He held the drone controller. "Look here," he said.

MK looked at the control monitor. The screen showed a balding man holding a black box, running through the fairgrounds. "Is that still recording?"

The smile on Buck's face stretched with great satisfaction. "Not only that, but check this out." Buck set the controller down and stepped into the main room. He grabbed a cell phone he had propped up on a bookshelf. "I also recorded what that maniac did in here." Buck pressed a button to stop recording. "I set it up right after I texted you. Thankfully, he was more interested in the 'evidence' than in what I was doing."

MK nodded with approval. "I could kiss you," MK gushed. "Well done, Buck."

The smile evaporated from Buck's face and his eyebrows rose in anticipation. MK considered following through with the reward, but opted against it. "Keep on him, Buck."

Buck scowled as he picked up the drone controller and continued following the Fair Thief. Then his attention shifted to a green golf cart racing behind the suspect. Fair patrons leapt from the path as the cart chased its prey. "Hey, MK. You might want to see this."

"Oh, Jenny," MK groaned. "I'm calling the police."

***

The balding man's chest heaved for breath. Sweat drenched his shirt and dripped from his forehead as he turned back to glance at the pursuing golf cart. He pushed his body beyond its normal limits and his wobbly legs felt like they would give out at any moment. Panting, he turned at the merry-go-round and prepared for the final, but arduous dash towards the south parking lot. He glanced again over his left shoulder, then his right, but the pursuing cart was gone. A weary smile attempted to form on his face, but his exhaustion wouldn't allow for cheer of any kind. His jog slowed to a fast walk as he scanned the alleys behind and to the side. Then, remembering the nearness of the parking lot, he quickened his pace.

Jenny slammed on the brakes and the golf cart slid to a stop mere feet in front of her prey. Still looking backwards, the man didn't see the cart and barreled right into it. The DVR box fell to the ground. Panting heavily, he bent over to pick it up, but collapsed to one knee.

"You're done, Tom," Jenny barked as she climbed out of the cart. She recognized the confusion on his face. "That's right, Tom Snelly. We know who you are and we know you stole the winning quilts from the show. We have the proof."

Tom picked up the DVR and held it to his chest like a beloved stuffed animal.

"Tom, I spoke to your grandmother, Judith. She's a sweet woman. She wouldn't approve of what you're doing," Jenny said. She walked around the back of the cart and towered over Tom who still rested on one knee. He stood slowly, but Jenny was taller. "You can still choose to do the right thing."

Tom sneered.

"The DVR is worthless, Tom. There's nothing on it. We set a trap and you fell for it. It's time to end this silliness."

Tom looked at the worthless black box clutched in his hands, and then at Jenny. Then at the driver's seat of the golf cart.

"Don't do it Tom. It's over," Jenny implored. "The police are on their way."

Without warning, Tom heaved the DVR at Jenny. She quickly stepped aside and the DVR sailed past her before slamming to the ground with a metallic thud. Then Tom spread his feet and lowered his shoulder like a football player preparing for a tackle. Jenny's eyes widened with alarm, but before Tom could attack, the drone swooped down from its position overhead. Seeing the drone out of the corner of her eye, Jenny crouched low as the drone dove and slammed into the side of Tom's head. He plummeted to the ground and sprawled spread eagle on his stomach. The drone lay in pieces beside him. Jenny leaned close and could see his breath disturbing the dusty ground. As Tom started to stir, Jenny knelt on his back to hold him in place. Her phone chirped and she pulled it from her back pocket.

"Police should be there any moment," MK said quickly. Just as MK said it, Jenny saw two uniformed officers racing toward her. Jenny stood, removing her knee from Tom's back. She placed the phone in her back pocket and held her empty hands open in front of her as the police arrived. "I'm making a citizen's arrest," Jenny said to the first officer at the scene.

The officer smiled politely as he eyed Jenny in all of her disheveled, dusty glory, and then Tom who was still prostrate on the ground. "Please back away, ma'am."

Jenny complied. "This is the man who stole the winning quilts from the Quilting Competition. He also assaulted me, maybe others."

"Don't forget the vandalism to the trailer," MK said loudly enough for both Jenny and the officer to hear from Jenny's back pocket.

The officers cuffed the Fair Thief and sat him in the golf cart until backup arrived. They took Jenny's full statement. MK and Buck arrived minutes later to give their statements as well. Finally, Stephanie approached the scene, a churro in one hand and a stack of fliers in the other.

"You did it," Stephanie gushed. "But …" She paused as she thought. "I hardly even got any of these fliers out to lure the thief. How …?" Stephanie walked around the golf cart and looked at the suspect. "Mr. Snelly?"

"You know him?" MK asked.

Stephanie thought. "No. Well, yes. Kind of. He works for the fair administration. He's the one who set us up with the trailer." Stephanie glared at Tom Snelly.

"Just wait until your grandma hears about this," MK said.

"Actually, that's a great idea," Jenny agreed. She dialed Judith and explained the situation. "Judy, you really can help us with something."

"Anything, Love," Judith said in her sweet southern accent. Moments later, with the speaker at full volume, Judith spoke kindly to her grandson. Then she said, "Heaven help me, Tommy. You'd best tell me where those quilts are and you'd better do it now."

Tommy Snelly obeyed his grandmother and the quilts were soon recovered from a storage room on the fairgrounds.

Jenny dusted off the dirt from her clothes and then turned to Stephanie. "It's been a pleasure." Both women smiled, and then hugged.

"MK, our work is done here and we still have time to catch our flight," Jenny said.

MK nodded in agreement. "Just one thing first." MK walked over to where Buck was standing. "Thank you, Buck. For everything. We couldn't have done this without you." MK leaned in and kissed Buck on the cheek. "It was nice meeting you."

Buck grinned from ear to ear and simply waved goodbye as Jenny and MK strolled away, off to their next adventure.